Beaver Valley Ontario in Colour Photos, Saving Our History One Photo at a Time

Photography
by Barbara Raué
2021

Series Name:
Cruising Ontario

Book 197: Clarksburg, Craigleith, Flesherton, Heathcote, Leith, Markdale, Meaford, Thornbury, Victoria Corners, Walter's Falls

Cover photo: Home in Flesherton

Series Name: Cruising Ontario
Saving Our History One Photo at a Time
in colour photos

Books Available in Alphabetical Order:
Aberfoyle, Acton, Alton, Amherstburg, Ancaster, Arthur, Aylmer, Ayr, Belleville, Bloomingdale, Brantford, Brockville, Burford, Burlington, Caledon, Caledonia, Cambridge, Clifford, Conestogo, Delhi, Dorchester to Aylmer, Drayton, Drumbo, Dundas, Eden Mills, Elmira, Elora, Erin, Essex, Fergus, Goderich, Guelph, Hagersville, Hamilton, Hanover, Harriston, Hespeler, Jarvis, Kingston, Kingsville, Kitchener, Lake Superior, Linwood, Listowel, London, Lucknow, Merrickville, Mono, Mount Forest, Neustadt, New Hamburg, Newboro, Newport Mt Pleasant, Niagara-on-the-Lake, Oakville, Onondaga, Orangeville, Orillia, Owen Sound, Palmerston, Paris, Perth, Peterborough, Petrolia, Port Colborne, Port Elgin, Portland, Preston, Rockwood, Sarnia, Sault Ste. Marie, Seaforth, Sheffield, Shelburne, Simcoe, Smiths Falls, Southampton, St. George, St. Jacobs, St. Marys, St. Thomas, Stoney Creek, Stratford, Thamesford, Thunder Bay, Tillsonburg, Waterdown, Waterford, Waterloo, Welland, Wellesley, Westport, Windsor, Wingham, Woodstock

Book 185-186: Grimsby
Book 187: Toronto
Book 188: Collingwood
Book 189-193: St. Catharines
Book 194: Smithville
Book 195: Town of Lincoln
Book 196: Town of Pelham
Book 197: Beaver Valley

Table of Contents

Beaver Valley

    Clarksburg

    Markdale

    Craigleith

    Flesherton

    Leith

    Heathcote

    Meaford

    Thornbury

    Victoria Corners

    Walter's Falls

Beaver Valley

The Beaver Valley is located in southern Ontario at the southern tip of Georgian Bay. The Beaver River flows north through the valley emptying into Georgian Bay in the town of Thornbury. It is a productive agricultural area producing 25% of Ontario's apple crop on 7,500 acres of apple orchards. The main towns in the valley from Flesherton at the south end are Kimberley and Thornbury. Grey Road 13 follows the meandering Beaver River along the valley floor. It rises briefly before crossing the river again at Heathcote.

Clarksburg

Clarksburg, the hidden gateway between the picturesque backroads of the Beaver Valley, the slopes of the Blue Mountains, and the shores of Georgian Bay, is located just south of Thornbury on Grey Road 13. The Beaver River cascades through a series of picturesque rapids from Clendenan Dam through the village and north to Georgian Bay. In 1858 William Jabez Marsh travelled from Holland Landing to purchase 500 acres of Crown land adjacent to the village of Thornbury. After choosing a location for his own farm, he donated 2.5 acres for the building of a church and rectory. The first church was a frame building erected in 1863 and named St. George's and was located in the newly established village of Clarksburg immediately adjacent to the border with Thornbury in order to serve both municipalities. The original church served until 1899 when it was replaced by the present brick structure erected on the same site. Once the brick church was completed, the original frame building was dismantled and transported in mid-winter by horse-drawn sleighs to Beaverdale where it was reassembled and continued to serve the congregation there for another 50 years. The brick rectory next to the church was built in 1867 and has been well maintained.

Markdale

Markdale is located on Highway 10 north of Flesherton. Settlement began in 1849, and it was incorporated as a village in 1888 with a thriving business center, three churches, a bank, a school, a wagon shop and a drug store. The beautiful Beaver Valley lies just a few miles to the east of Markdale.

Craigleith

Craigleith is located east of Thornbury on Georgian Bay. The name is Gaelic meaning rocky bay and the town was given the name by Andrew Craig Fleming, one of the community's earliest settlers. Craigleith was the home of Sir Sandford Fleming who contributed to the establishment of standard time earning him the title of "The Father of Standard Time." Fleming also designed the first Canadian postage stamp; issued in 1851, it cost three pennies and depicted the beaver, now the national animal of Canada. The Sanford family began operating a quarry and lumber mill in Craigleith which provided essential building materials to their new settlement.

On November 24, 1872 the steamer "Mary Ward" ran aground two kilometers offshore as she was travelling from Sarnia to Collingwood. A group of local fishermen rescued those remaining on board; however, the last of three rescue boats capsized and eight passengers drowned.

One of the last remaining wooden CNR stations is located here.

Flesherton

Flesherton is located at the junction of Highway 10 and Grey County Road 4. In 1850, 25-year-old William Kingston Flesher surveyed a portion of the Township of Artemesia. The north-south Toronto-Sydenham Road and east-west Durham Road which both ran through the township, were built shortly after the survey was finished, thereby opening the area to settlement. The intersection of the two roads which lay in a small valley was named Artemesia Corners.

As was usual for the time, Flesher was paid for his work in property within the survey area. He chose the valley containing Artemesia Corners and laid out a portion in village lots. Aaron Munshaw arrived as the first settler and built a tavern on the southeast corner of the intersection of the two roads. In 1864 as the village grew, Munshaw built a larger inn and stagecoach stop that incorporated some parts of the original hotel. This building, operated as a hotel by the Munshaw family until the 1960s, is now known as Munshaw House and still stands on the original spot.

Throughout the 1850s many Scottish immigrants arrived to claim lots and began to clear the land. Mr. Flesher continued to develop the valley economy building a sawmill and a grist mill on the Boyne River that flowed through the bottom of the valley. He encouraged other businesses to settle in the area. In his honor, the name of the settlement was changed to Flesherton.

The red brick Methodist Church was built in 1877. In 1879 Chalmers Presbyterian Church was built where the Toronto-Sydenham Road crossed the Boyne River. In 1926 the Methodist Church joined with Chalmers Presbyterian to form St. John's United Church. The combined congregation chose to retain the highly visible Methodist building and sold the much smaller Presbyterian building.

Leith

Leith, located on the south shore of Georgian Bay, is nine kilometers northeast of the city of Owen Sound. It is the boyhood home of the renowned Canadian landscape artist Tom Thomson who is buried in the pioneer cemetery behind Leith United Church.

Heathcote

Heathcote is located in Grey County on the Beaver Road and Concession Road 13 south of Thornbury. William Fleming settled here in the 1840s and for a time the place was called Williamstown after him. That name was already in use elsewhere in Ontario, so when the post office opened in 1859, this community was called Heathcote, possibly after a place of that name in Derbyshire, England.

Meaford

Meaford is located on the southern shore of Georgian Bay, on Highway 26 between Thornbury and Owen Sound. In 1837 inhabitants of St. Vincent Township petitioned the government requesting that land at the mouth of the Bighead River be reserved as a landing place. In 1841 there was a saw mill, a grist mill, several roads had been constructed to the landing place, and a post office was established. The town plot of Meaford was laid out in 1845.

Meaford Town Hall was built in 1908-09 with Palladian lines and stately Doric columns after the original building built in 1864 had become dilapidated and was destroyed by fire on October 5, 1907. Local contractor James Sparling recycled as much of the original town hall's brick as possible in the construction of the new building. Like many public buildings across small-town Ontario, Meaford Hall was made to be more than a town hall. The building housed the council chambers and town offices. The chambers also served as a court room and there were two tiny jail cells in the basement.

At the other end of the building was the Meaford Public Library. Farmers used the basement on market day, and the space has been used for a ballroom, meeting area, and Boy Scouts hall. It has housed the Women's Institute, the Meaford Quilters, a Senior Citizens' Club, and the Senior Men's Euchre club. The second floor Opera House was the cultural heart of the community. Local plays, high school graduations, concerts and famous speakers have all made use of the theatre. In 1967, the library moved to a bigger space in the old post office. The Meaford Police Department left the hall in 1996. The town vacated the old offices in 2002.

In 2003, Meaford secured a grant to restore and renovate the building. Thousands of volunteer hours later, the Meaford Hall Arts and Cultural Centre opened for business in the spring of 2006. The building housing the current museum was built in 1895 as the towns Pumping Station. The Public Utilities Department was later relocated to the Pump House and the building was called the "Power House." During the 1940s, the chimney was removed. Cyrus Sing, a local citizen, donated his collection of memorabilia to the Town, and the building which had been vacant for a while was converted to a museum and opened to the public on July 1, 1961. Due to a continually expanding collection, several renovations and additions have been made to the building over the years.

Born in Nova Scotia, Margaret Marshall Saunders (1861-1947) was a novelist whose second book "Beautiful Joe" achieved international recognition. Inspired by a visit to Meaford in 1892, it is based on the story of a dog rescued from a brutal master by a local miller, William Moore. In 1994 the Beautiful Joe Heritage Society was formed to honor the life and story of Beautiful Joe and the literary and humane achievements of Margaret Saunders. Beautiful Joe Park is located in Meaford.

Victoria Corners

Victoria Corners is located on 21st Sideroad near Loree Forest and north of the hamlet of Banks.

Thornbury

Thornbury is located on Georgian Bay between Meaford and Collingwood. The Township of Thornbury was incorporated in 1833. In 1855 the town's first business, a milling operation, was set up, followed by a general store, blacksmith, cooper and fanning mill shops, grist and saw mills, and a post office. In 1887, feeling they were unfairly burdened with high taxes, the businessmen of Thornbury petitioned for independence from the Town of Collingwood. After much negotiating, they received it and the Township of Thornbury became the Town of Thornbury. The apple packing industry took root in Thornbury in 1885. At the Thornbury Village Cider House, they produce Premium Apple Cider from apples grown in the area, cider that is light, crisp and refreshing.

On January 1, 2001, the Town of Thornbury and the small settlements in the Township of Collingwood were amalgamated. Thornbury is the primary population center. The town's territory includes the communities of Banks, Camperdown, Castle Glen Estates, Christie Beach, Clarksburg, Craigleith, Duncan, Gibraltar, Heathcote, Kolapore, Little Germany, Lora Bay, Loree, Ravenna, Red Wing, Slabtown and Victoria Corners.

Walter's Falls

Walter's Falls is located south of Owen Sound on Grey County Road 29. It was the site of a saw mill and woolen mill. The saw mill burned down but the woolen mill remains. Water from Walter's Creek flows to form Walter's Falls.

Clarksburg

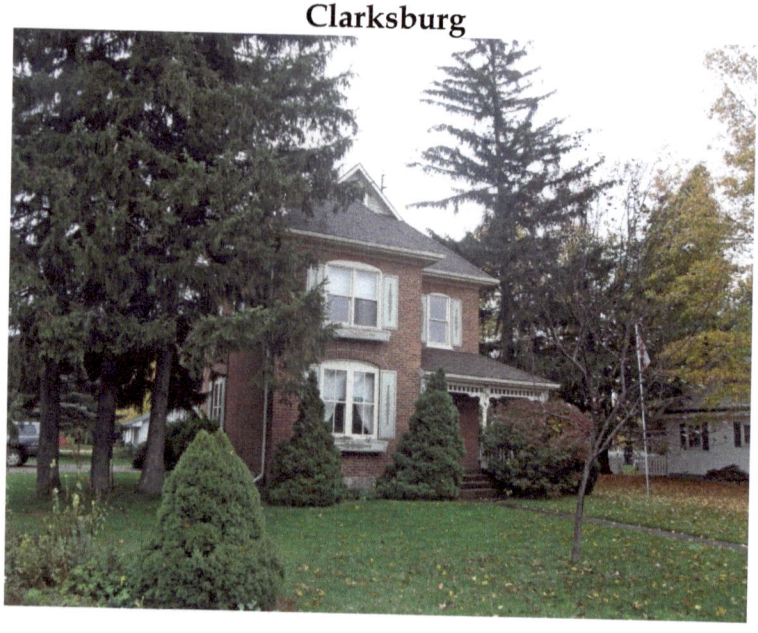

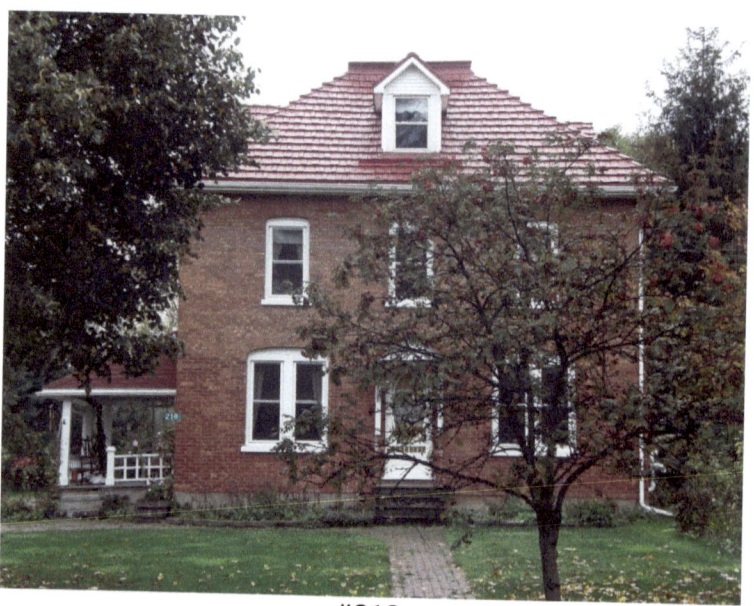

#218

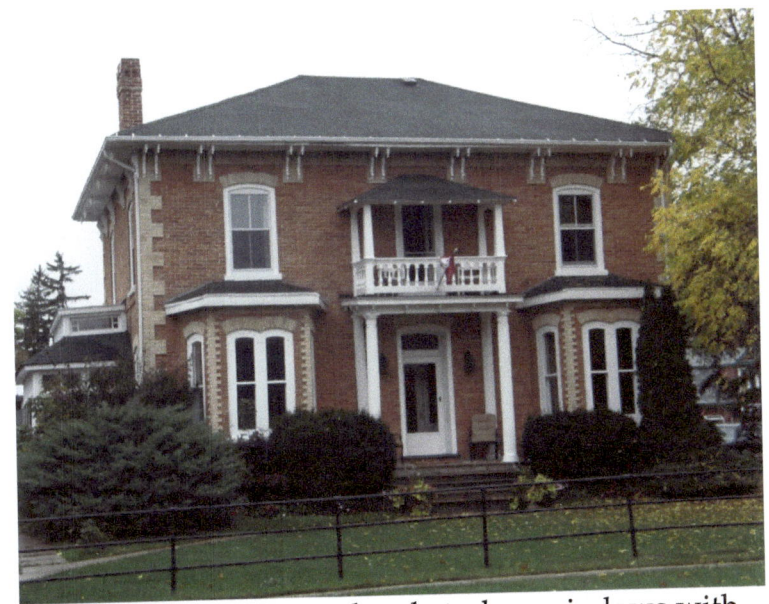

Hipped roof, paired cornice brackets, bay windows with corner quoins, second floor balcony

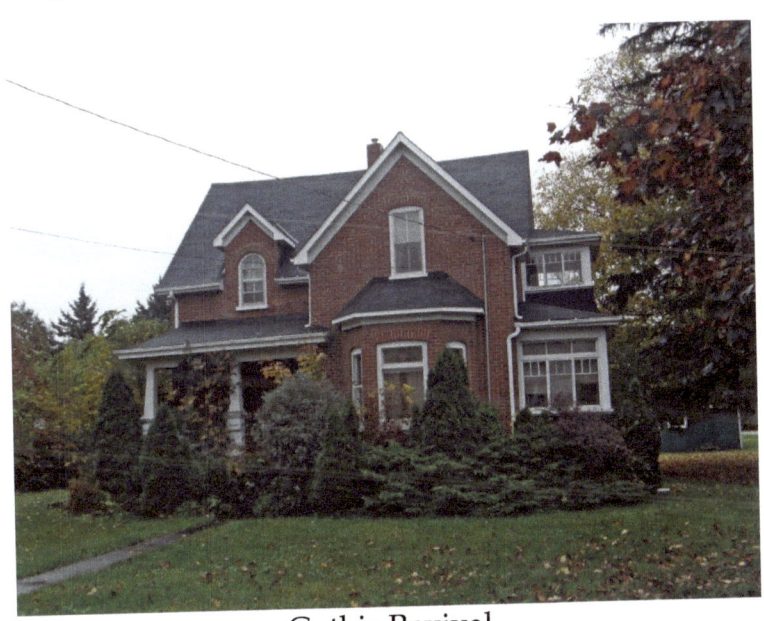

Gothic Revival

Clarksburg

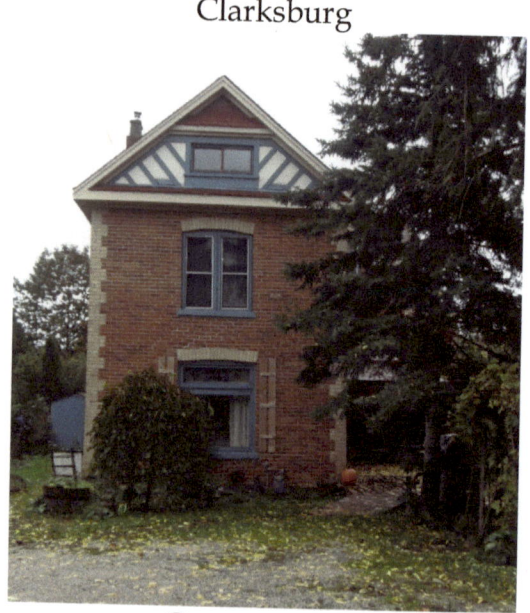

Corner quoins

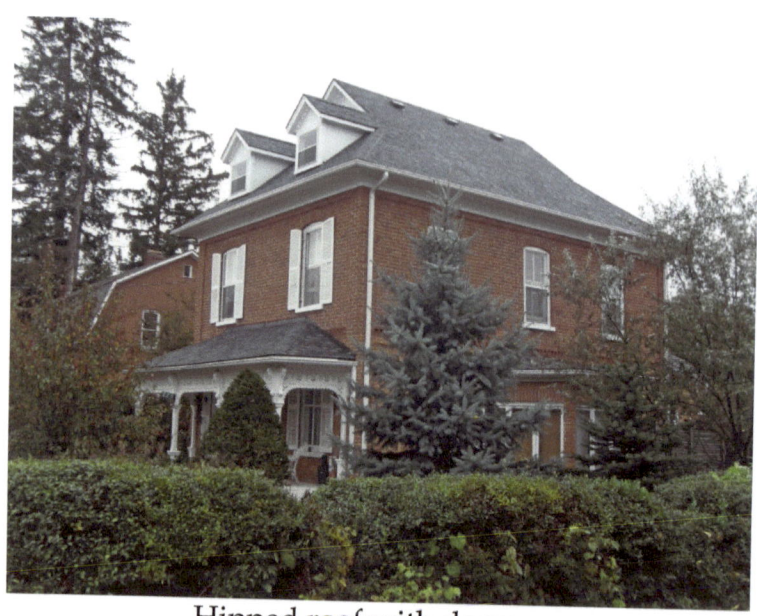

Hipped roof with dormers

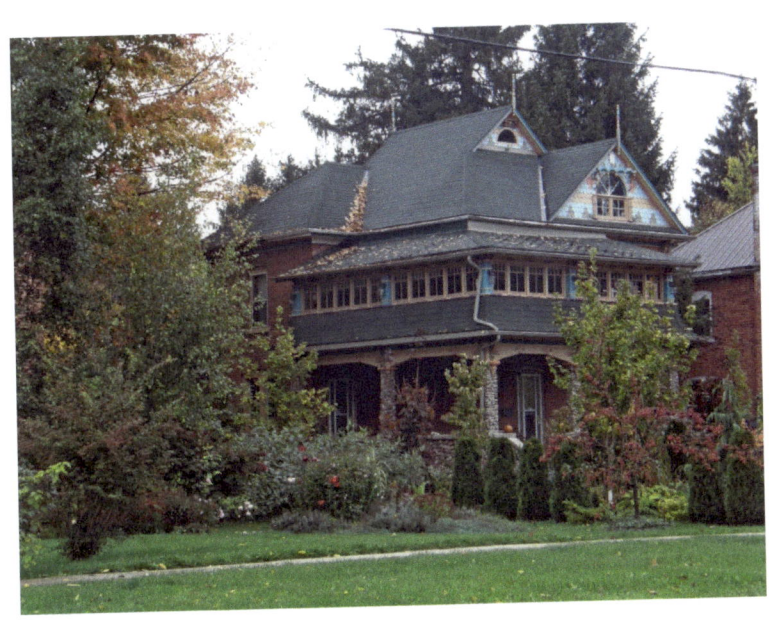

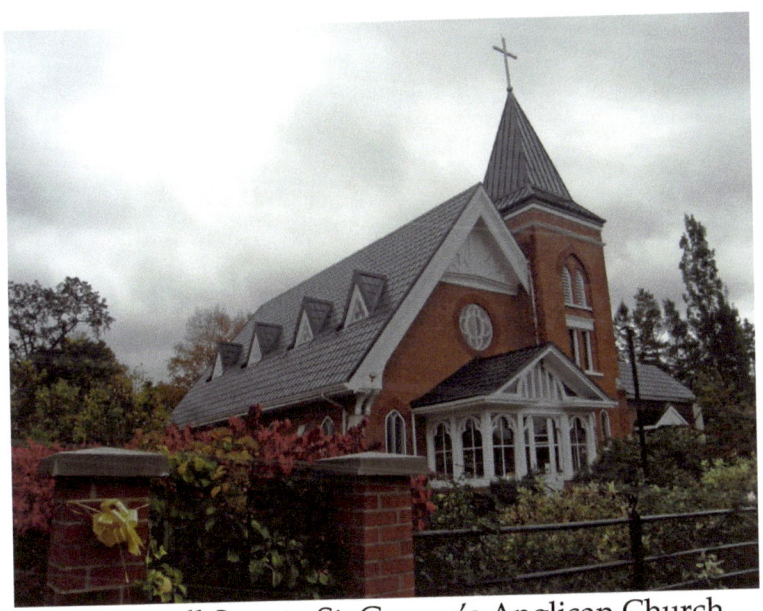

166 Russell Street - St. George's Anglican Church

Clarksburg

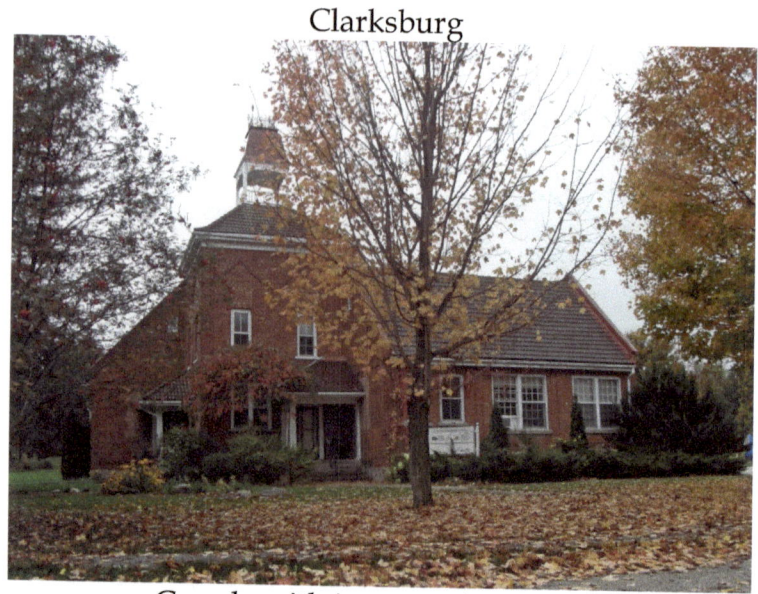

Cupola with iron cresting on top

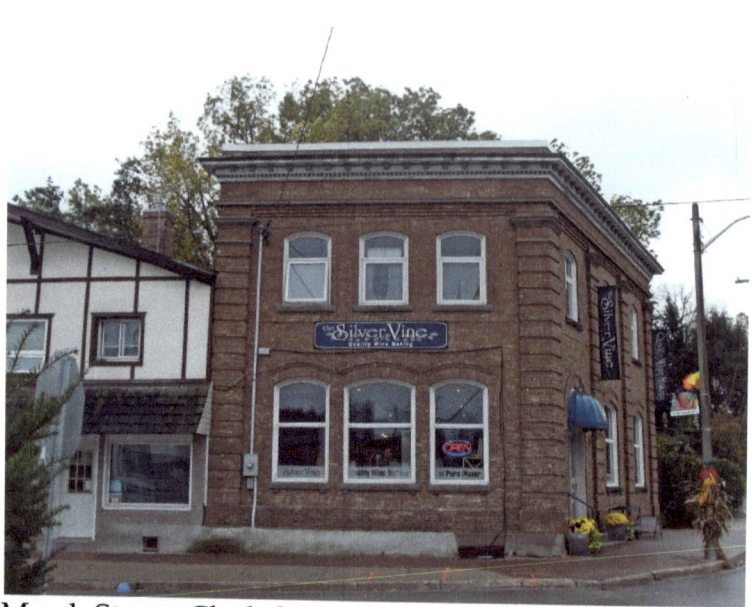

175 Marsh Street, Clarksburg - cornice brackets, dentil molding – The Silver Vine Winemaking

Craigleith

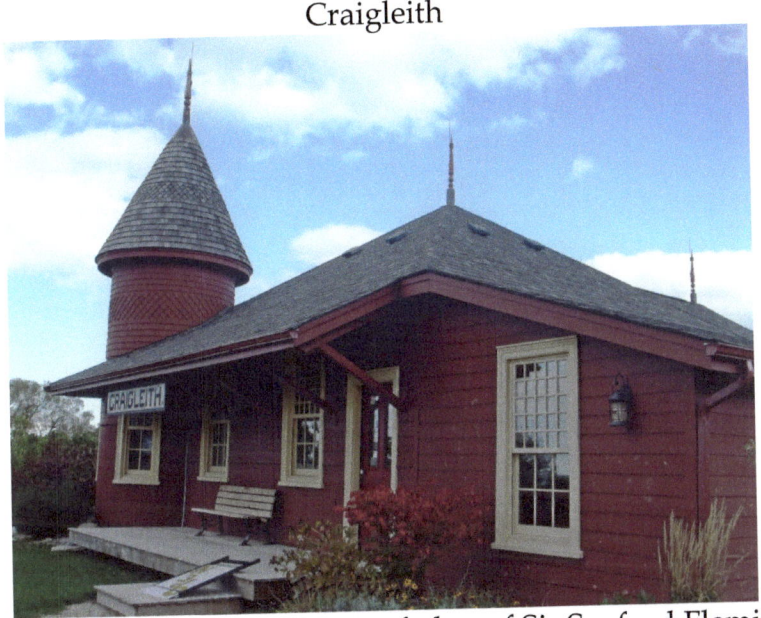

In 1872 Andrew Grieg Fleming, father of Sir Sanford Fleming, sold a parcel of land to the Northern Railway Company for the purpose of building a train station to serve his newly founded community. The station building was constructed from local timber between 1878 and 1881 and included a rounded turret. By 1881 there were six trains a day at the Craigleith station. In 1882, the Northern Railway was purchased by the Grand Trunk Railway. In 1923 the Grand Trunk became part of the Canadian National Railway. The convenience of the railway allowed businesses to be created and to prosper. In the 1940s the ski industry in Ontario began to grow with weekend ski trains from Toronto. Passenger service to the Craigleith station ended in 1960. In 1966 the station and lilac grove were saved from destruction by Kenn and Suyrea Knapman who re-opened the station as a restaurant and museum. In 2001 the Craigleith Depo was purchased by The Blue Mountains.

Markdale

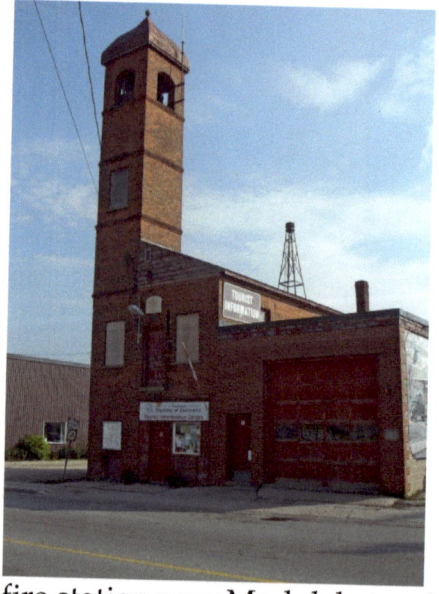

Historic fire station now Markdale tourist office

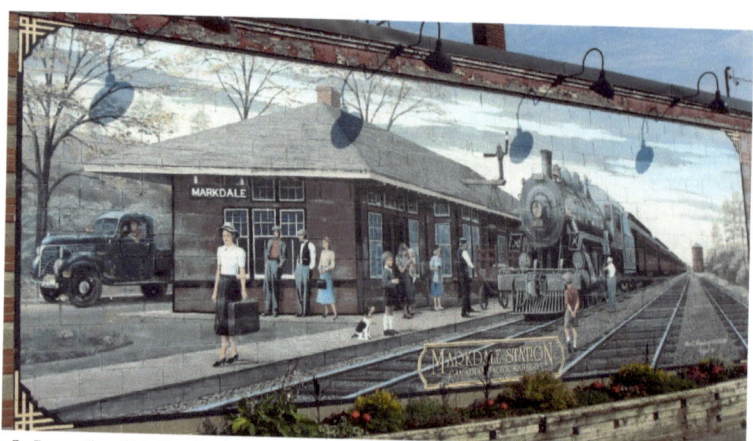

Mural of Markdale Canadian Pacific Railway Station

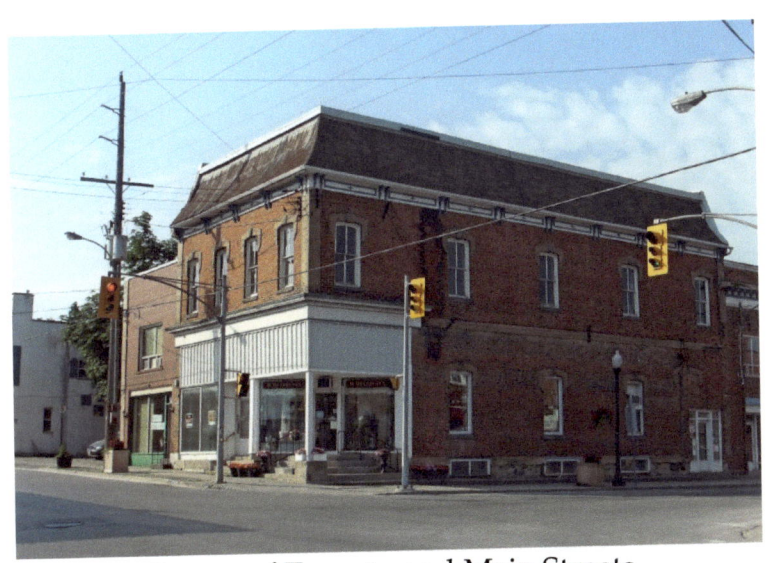

Corner of Toronto and Main Streets

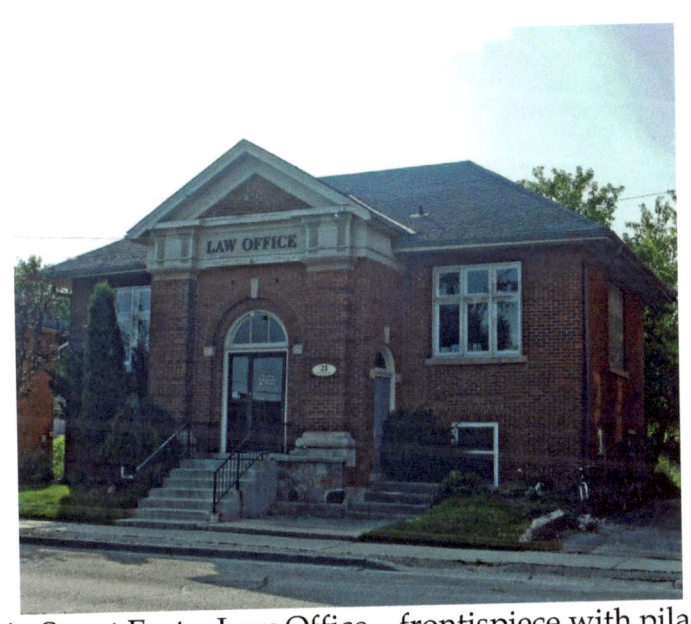

21 Main Street East – Law Office – frontispiece with pilasters topped by a pediment

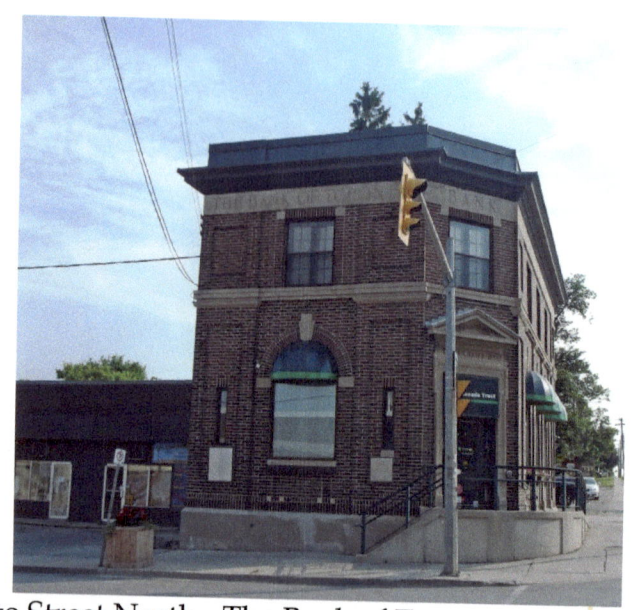

5 Toronto Street North - The Bank of Toronto, incorporated 1855 – now Canada Trust – voussoirs and keystone, pediment above entrance

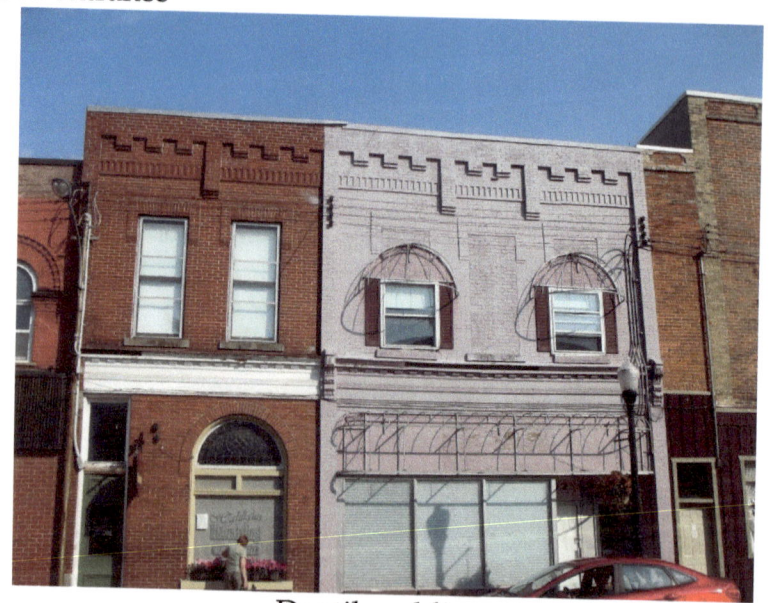

Dentil molding

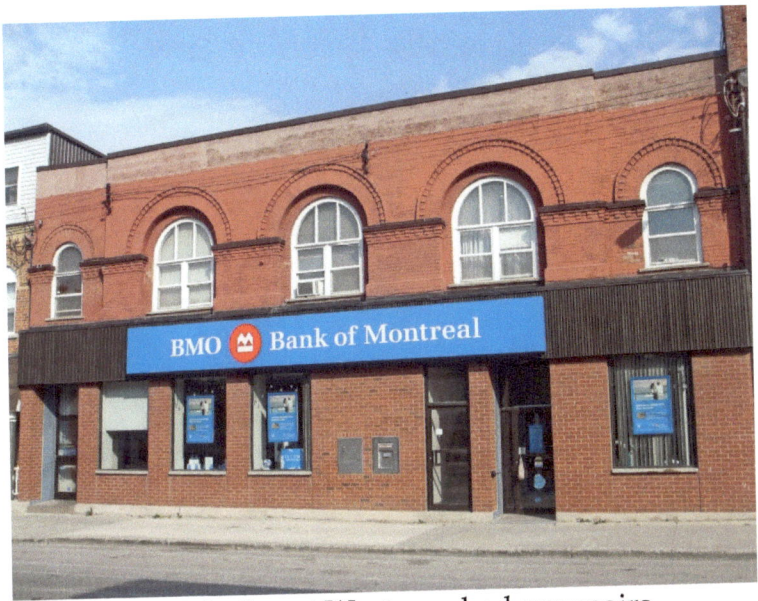

30 Main Street West - arched voussoirs

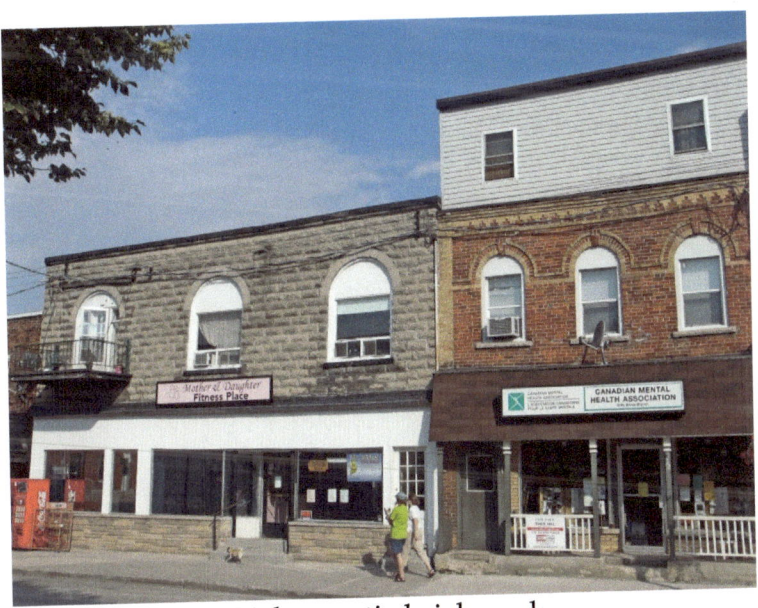

Dichromatic brickwork

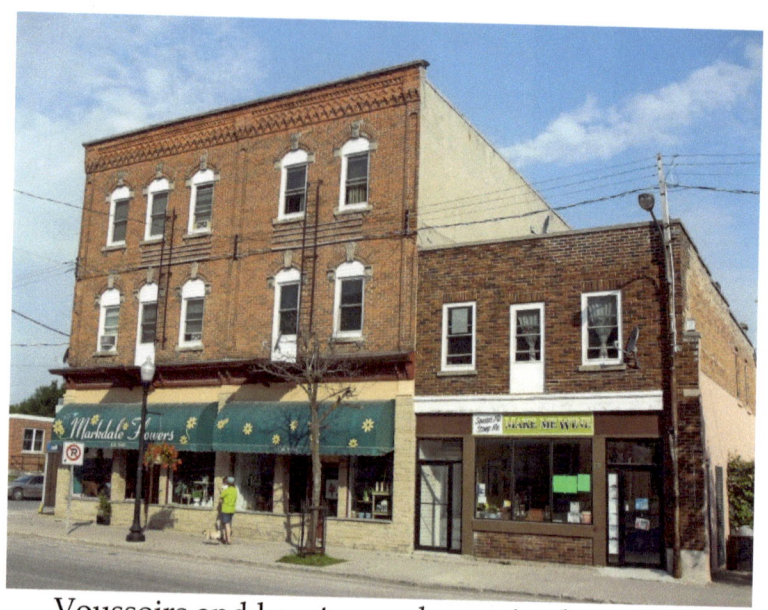
Voussoirs and keystones, decorative brickwork

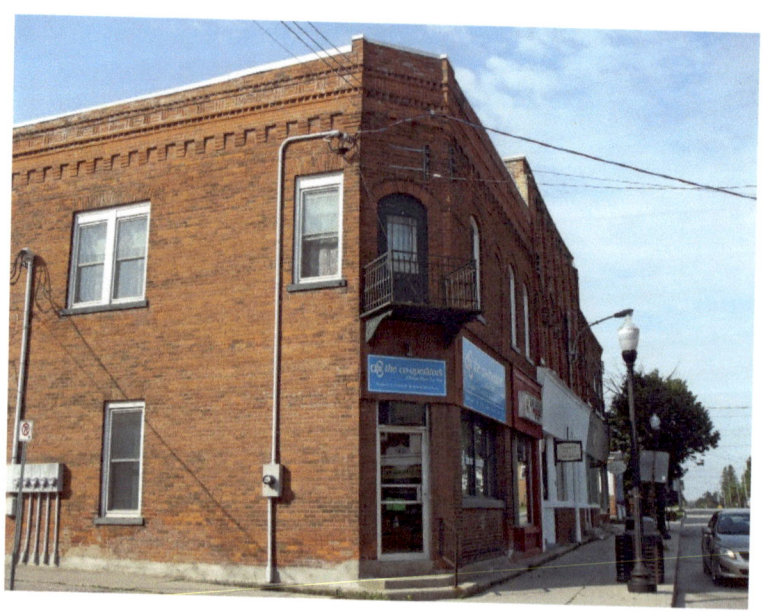

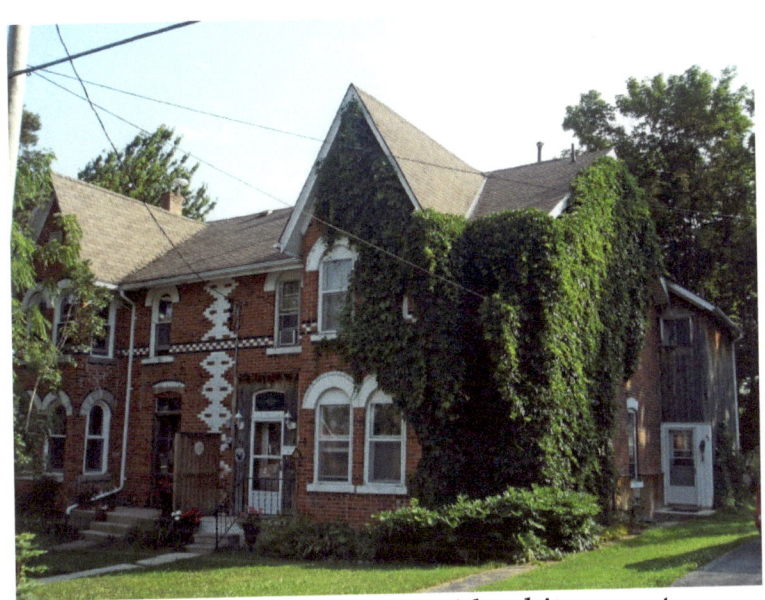

#41 - red brick Gothic style house with white accents, checkerboard band

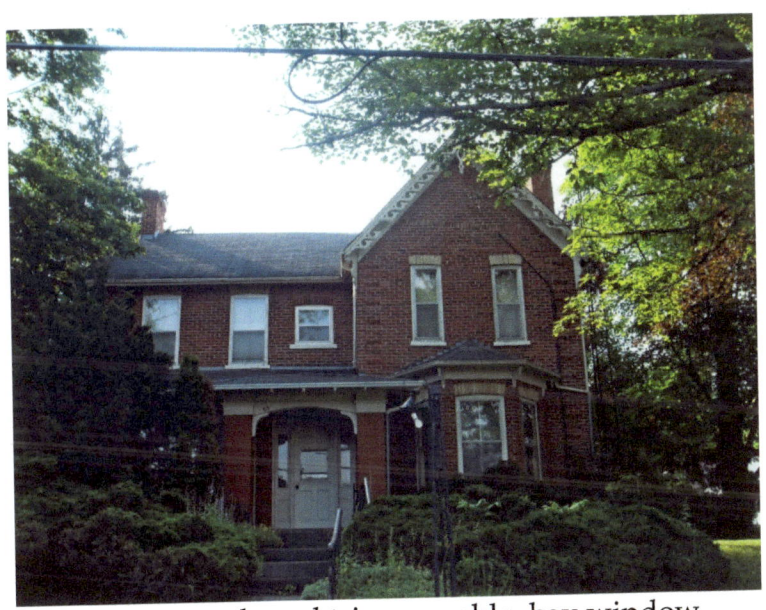

#65 - verge board trim on gable, bay window

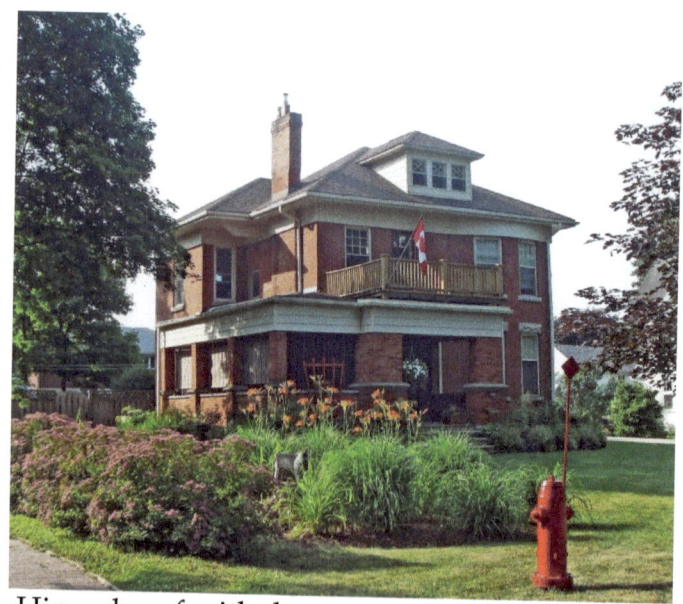
Hipped roof with dormer, second floor balcony

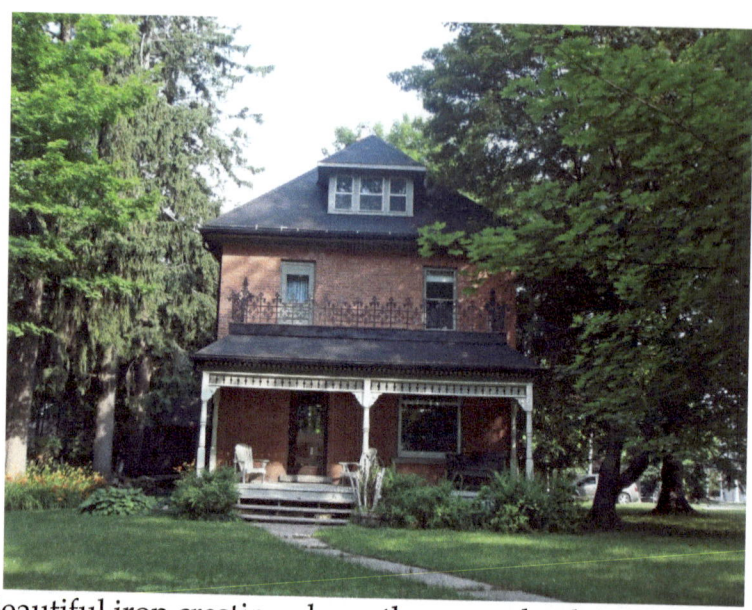
Beautiful iron cresting above the veranda, dormer in attic

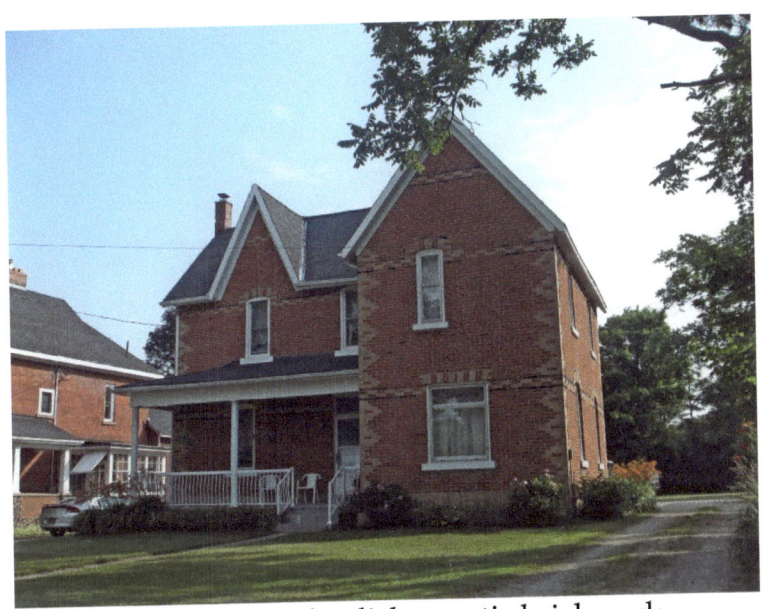

Gothic Revival – dichromatic brickwork

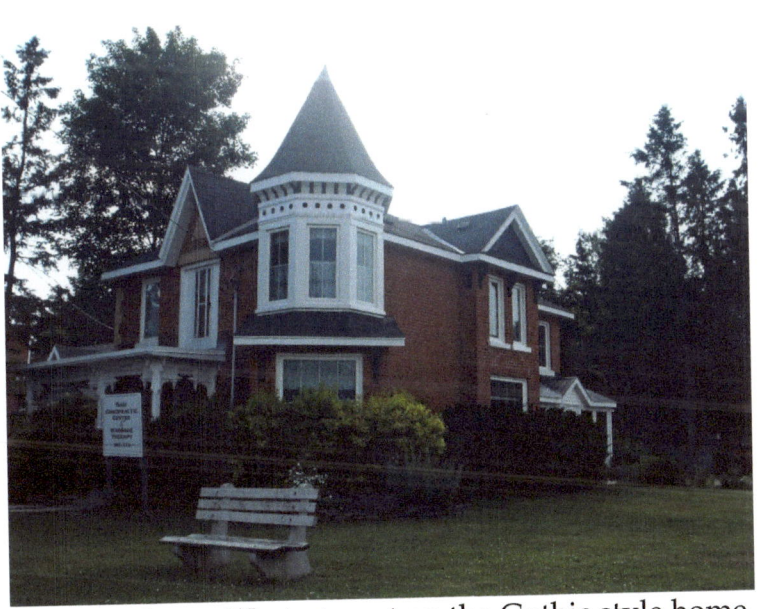

65 Main Street West - turret on the Gothic style home

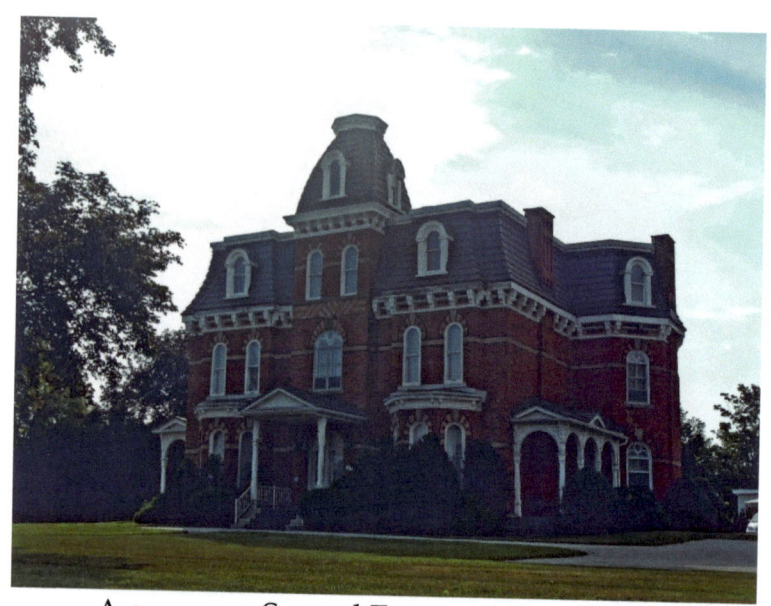

A gorgeous Second Empire style mansion

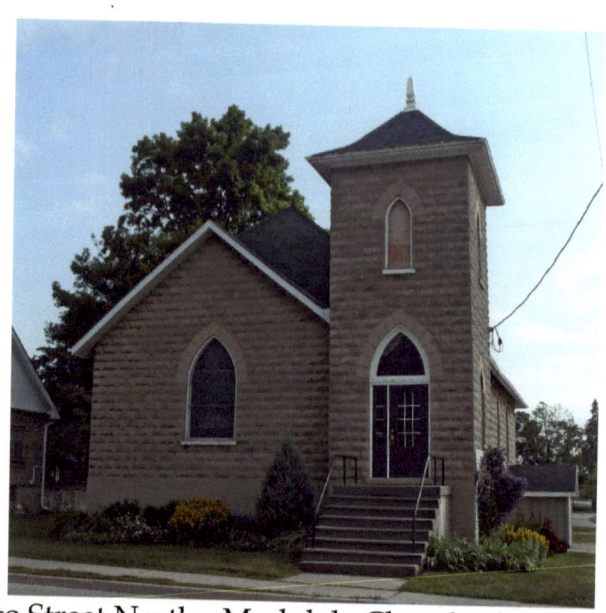

61 Toronto Street North - Markdale Church of the Nazarene – two-story tower, lancet windows

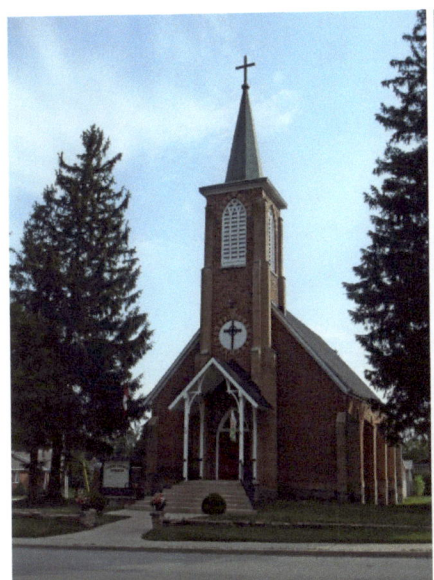
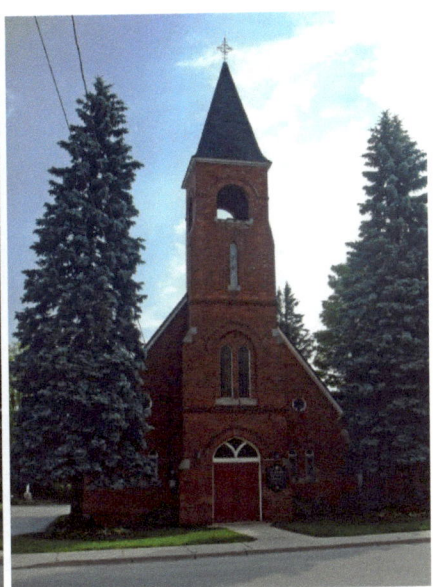

70 Toronto Street South
Christ Church Anglican
Dichromatic voussoirs,
buttresses

85 Toronto Street South
St. Joseph's Catholic Church
small rose windows on
either side of tower

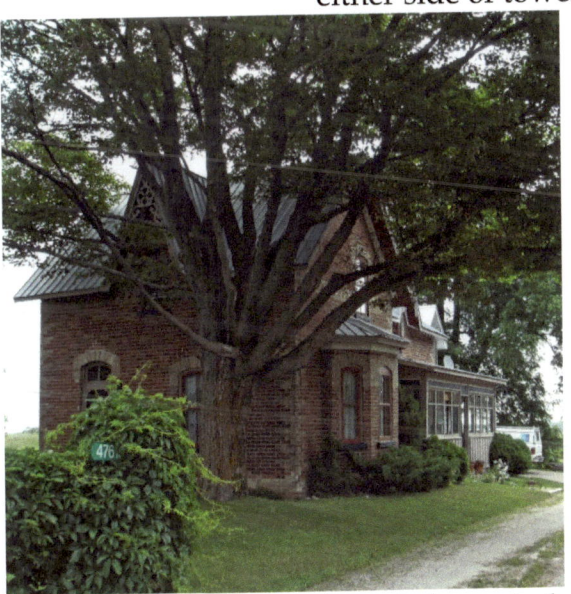

Gothic – dichromatic brickwork, bay window

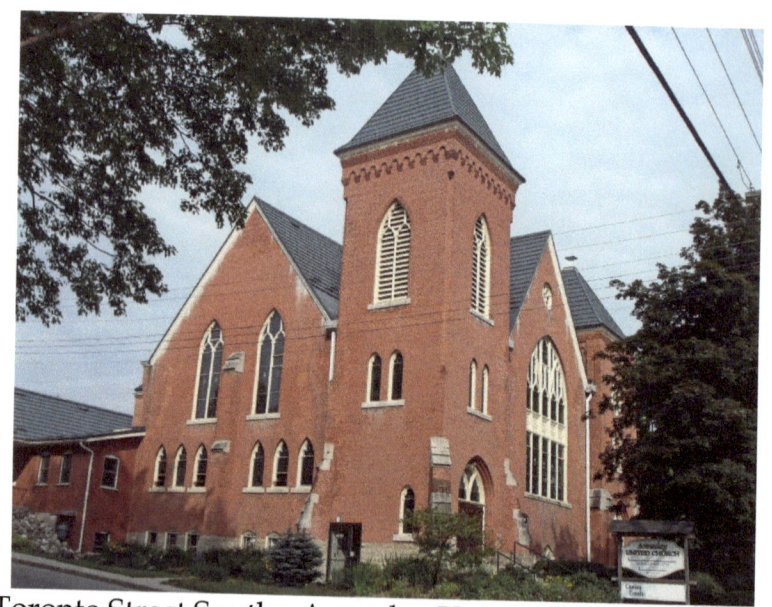

82 Toronto Street South - Annesley United Church Markdale – Gothic style, lancet windows with muntins, beveled dentil molding, buttresses

Flesherton

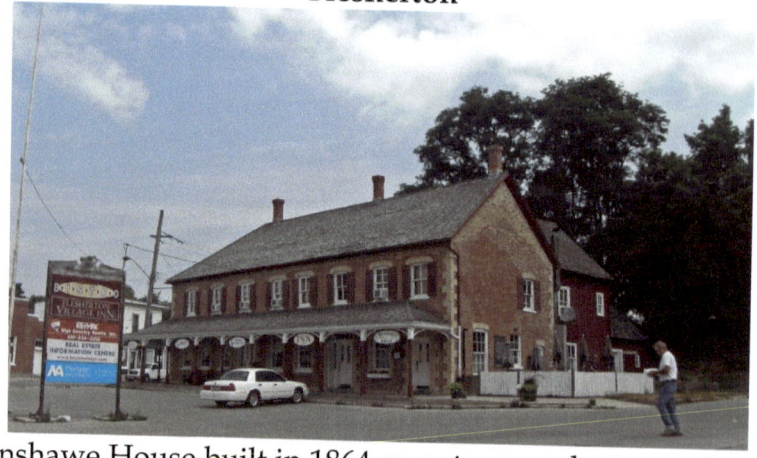

Munshawe House built in 1864 as a stagecoach stop at the junction of Toronto-Sydenham Road and Durham

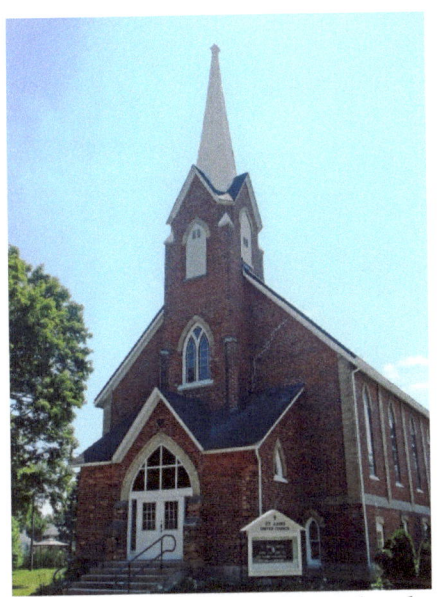

13 Spring Street - St. John's United Church – built in 1877 as the Methodist Church – lancet windows, tower with spire

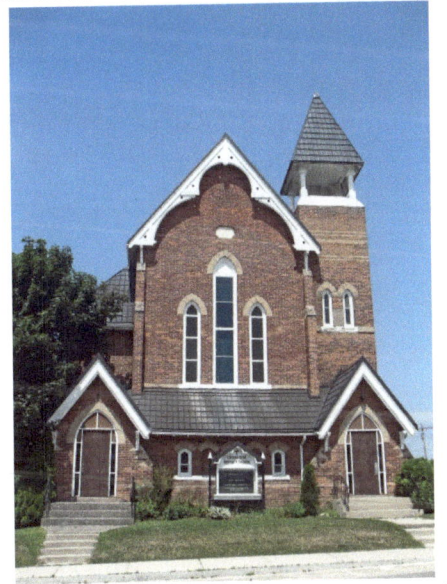

46 Collingwood Street - In 1886 Cedarside Baptist Church was built at the east end of the village. It has lancet windows, verge board trim on the gable, and a bell tower

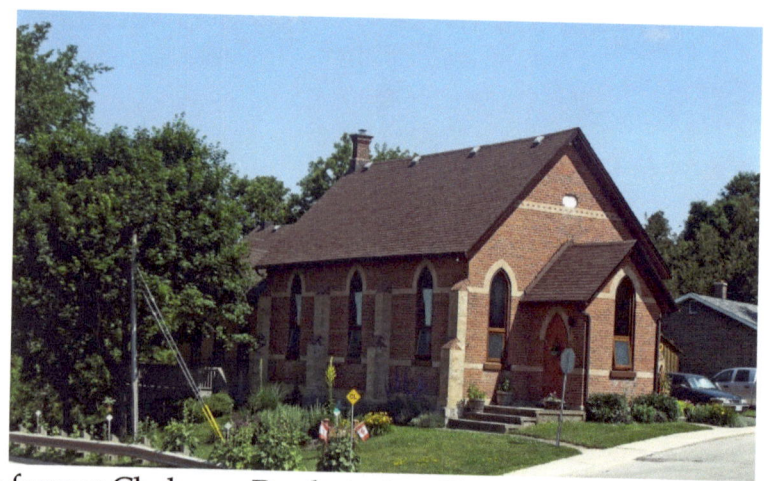

The former Chalmers Presbyterian Church built in 1879 – dichromatic brickwork, buttresses

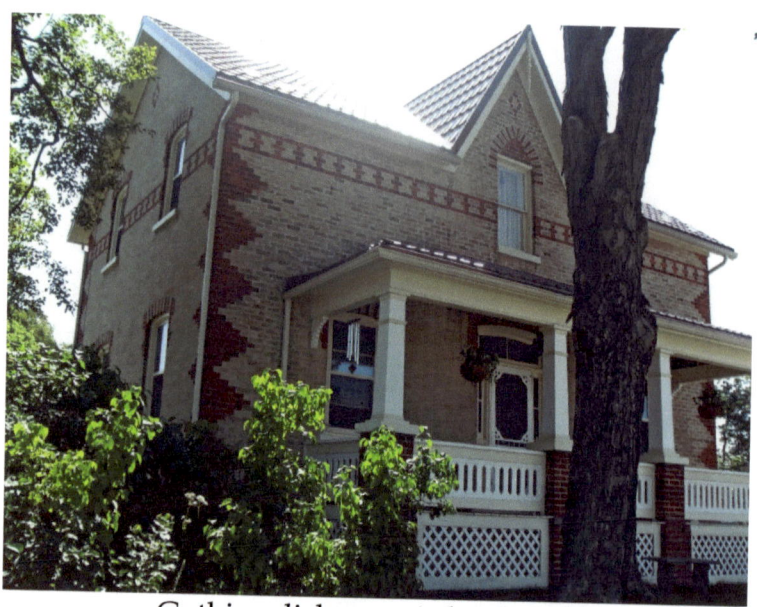

Gothic - dichromatic brickwork

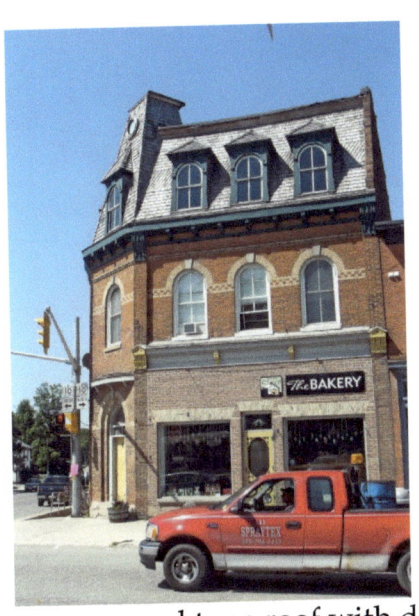

6 Sydenham Street - mansard type roof with dormers, cornice brackets, dichromatic brickwork

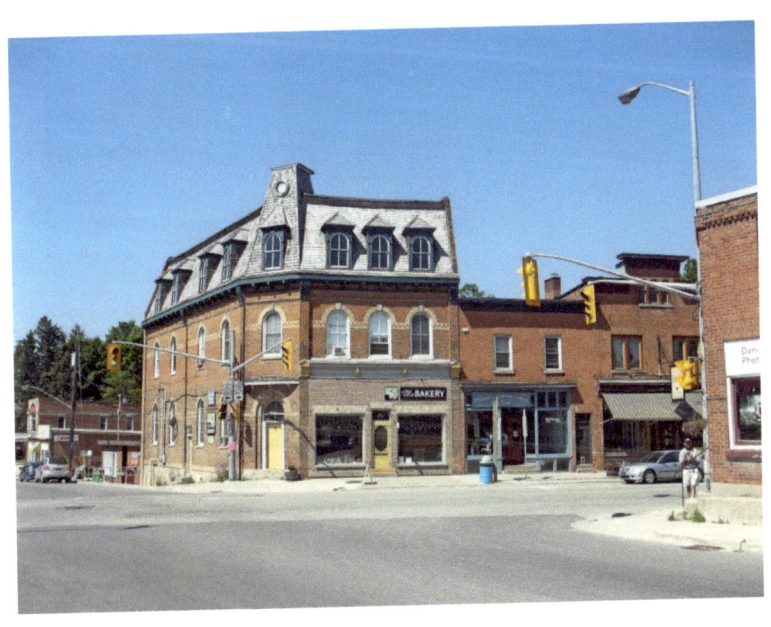

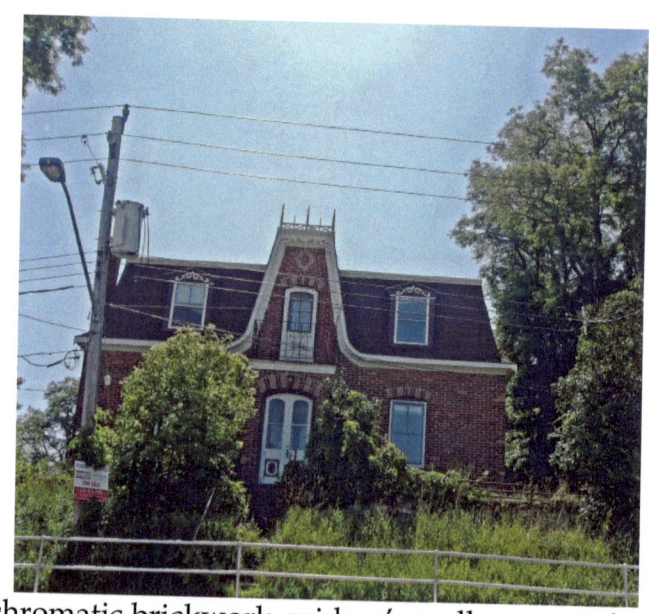

Dichromatic brickwork, widow's walk on top of gable

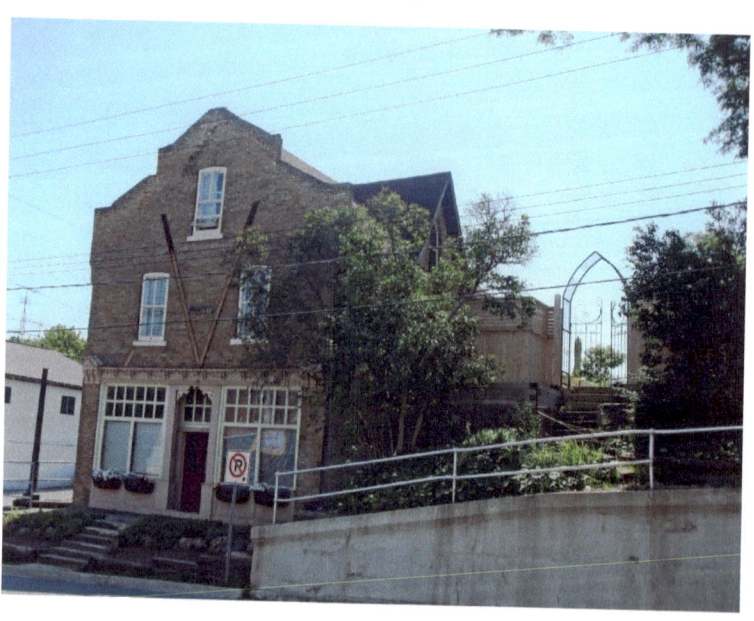

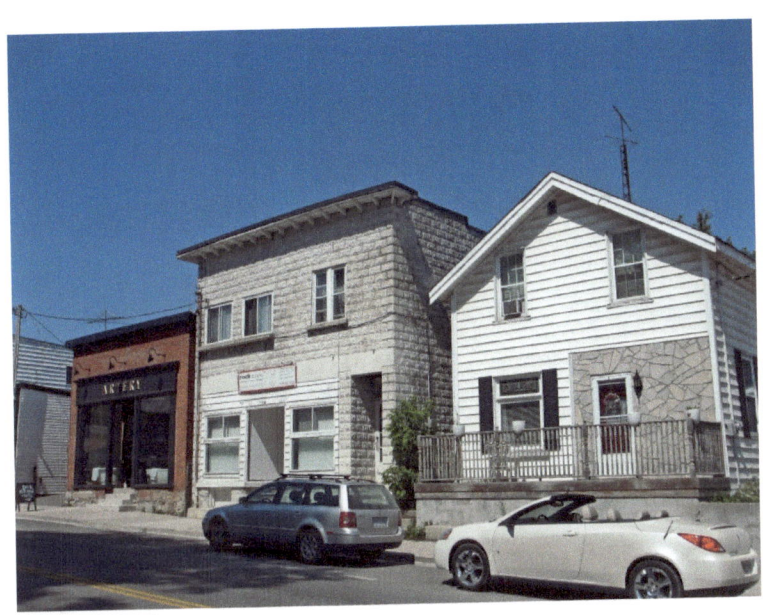
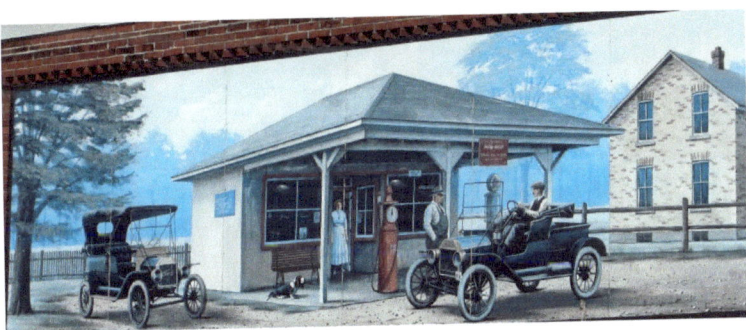
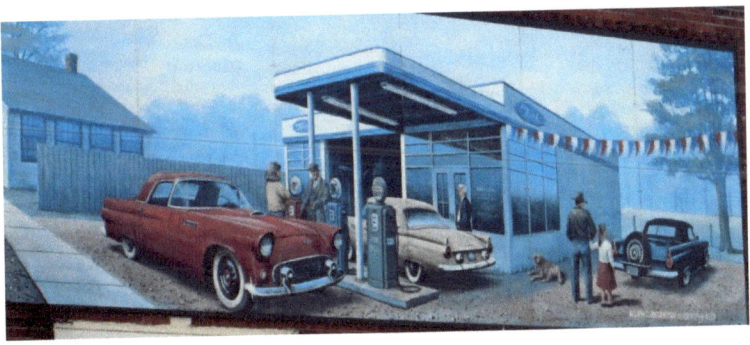

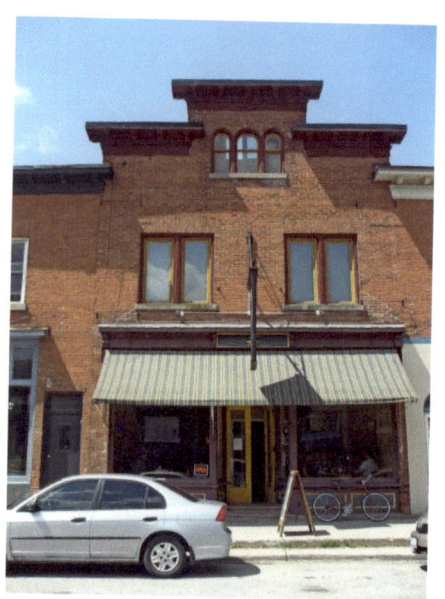

Stepped parapet

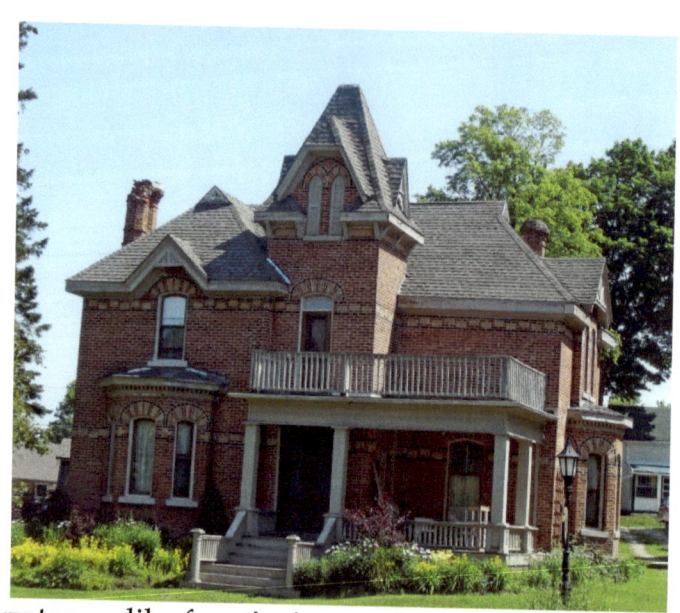

2½-story tower-like frontispiece, polychromatic brickwork and banding, bay windows, second floor balcony

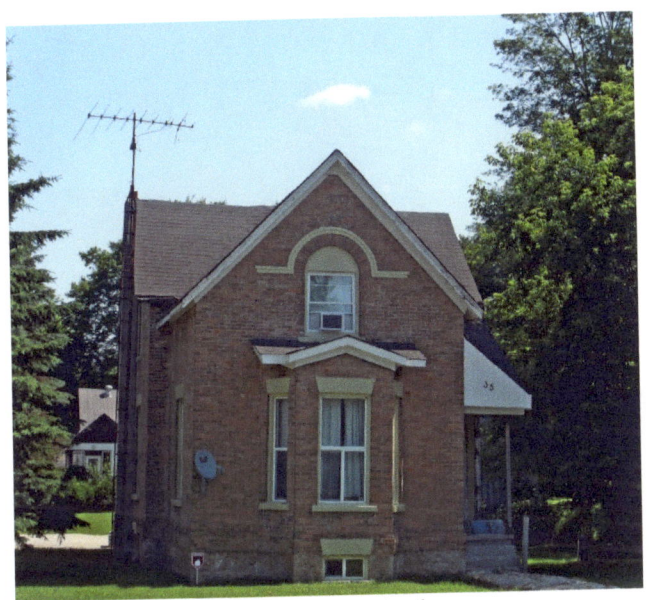

Gothic, bay window

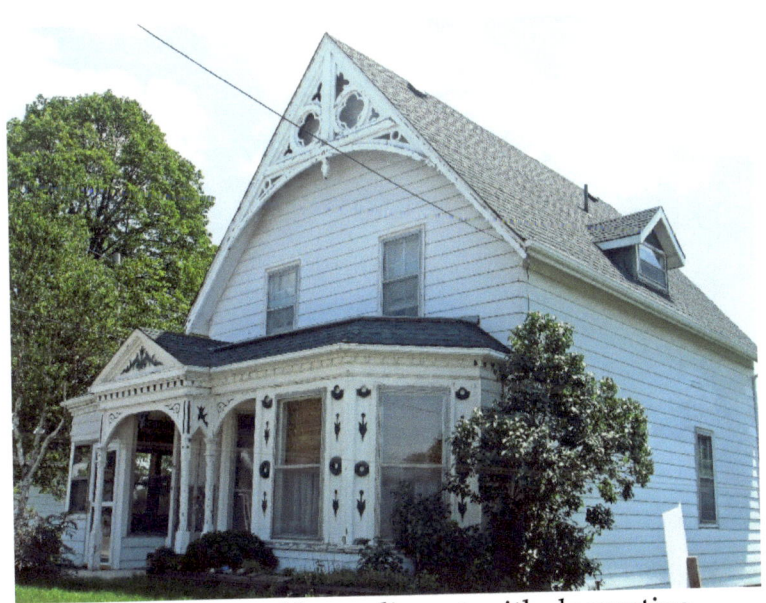

Verge board trim on gable, pediment with decorative tympanum

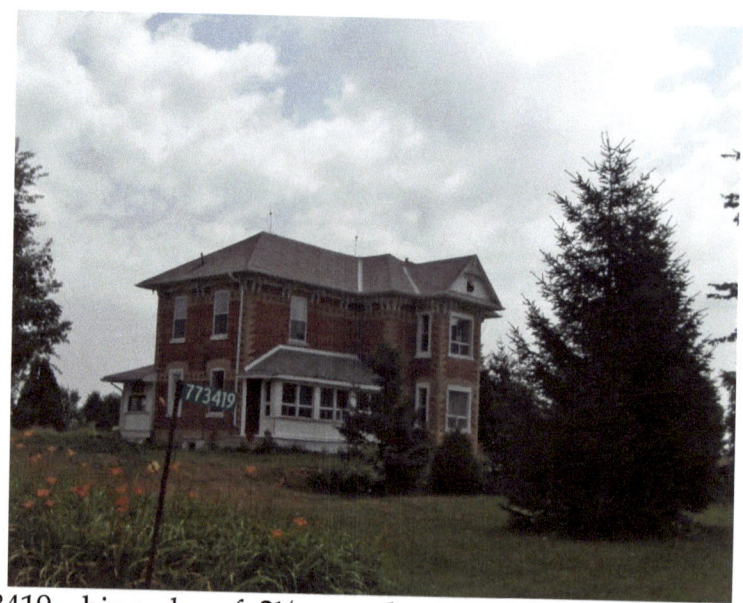

#773419 – hipped roof, 2½-story bay, cornice brackets, dichromatic brickwork

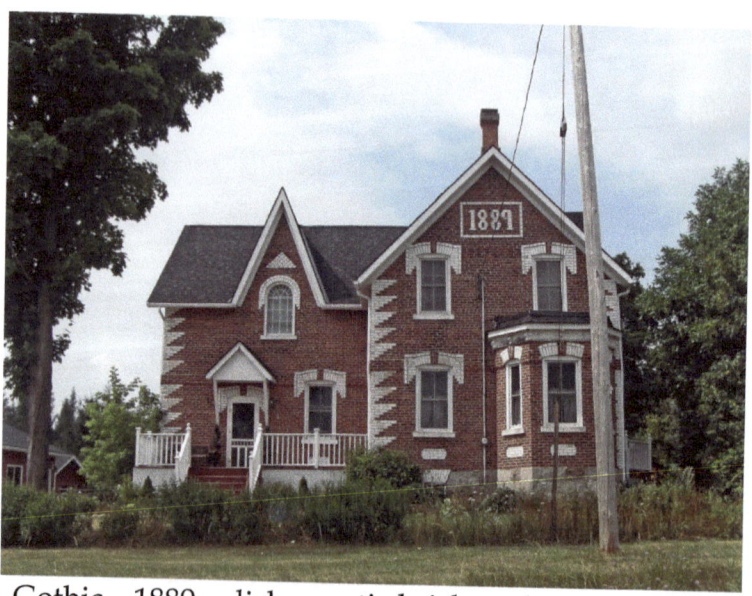

Gothic – 1889 – dichromatic brickwork, bay window

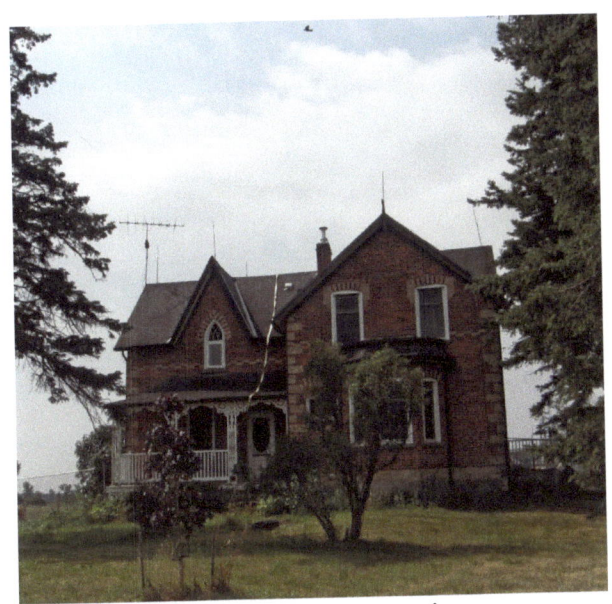

Gothic – corner quoins

Leith

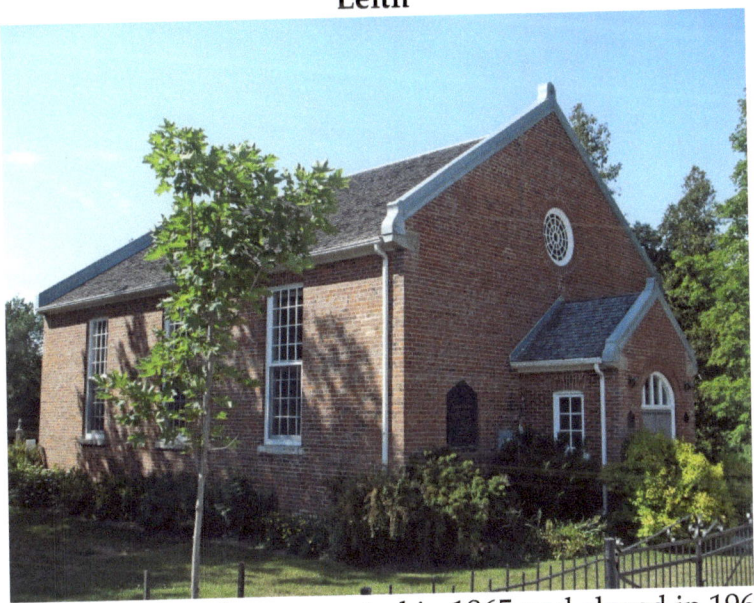

Leith United Church was erected in 1865 and closed in 1969. Since 1992 the church has been maintained by volunteers and is occasionally opened for special events.

Heathcote

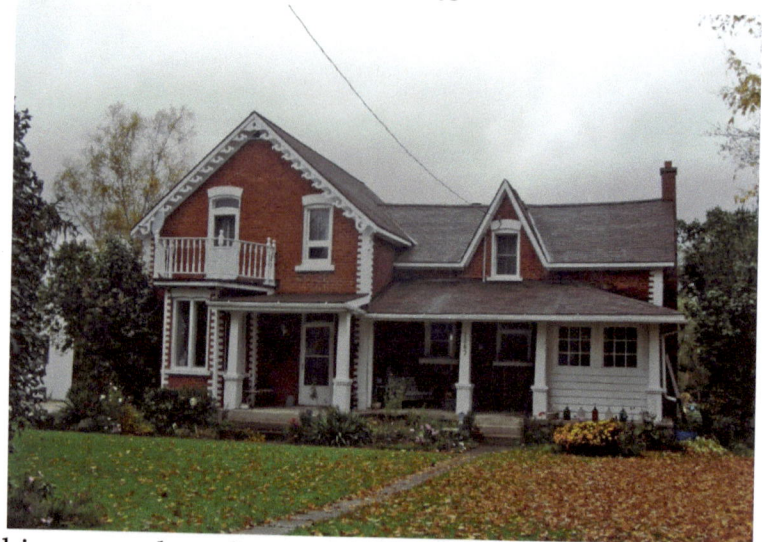

Gothic – verge board trim on large gable, second floor balcony

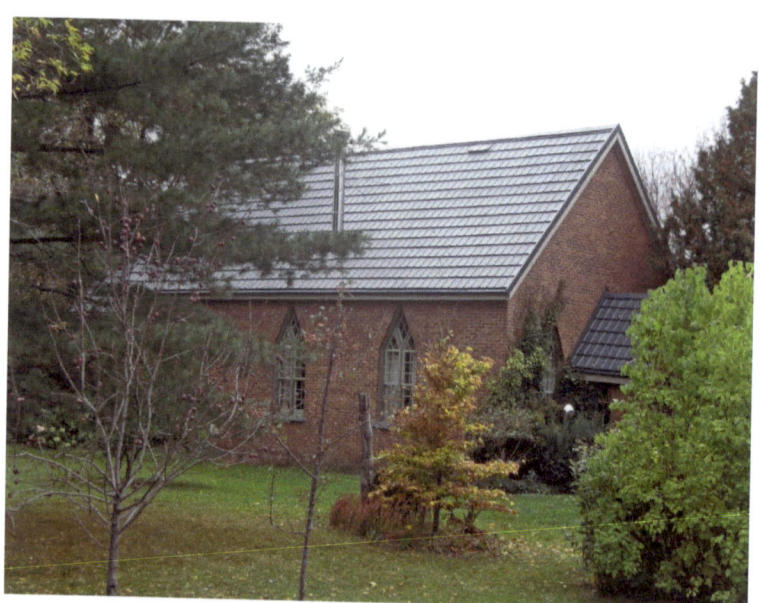

Marsh Street

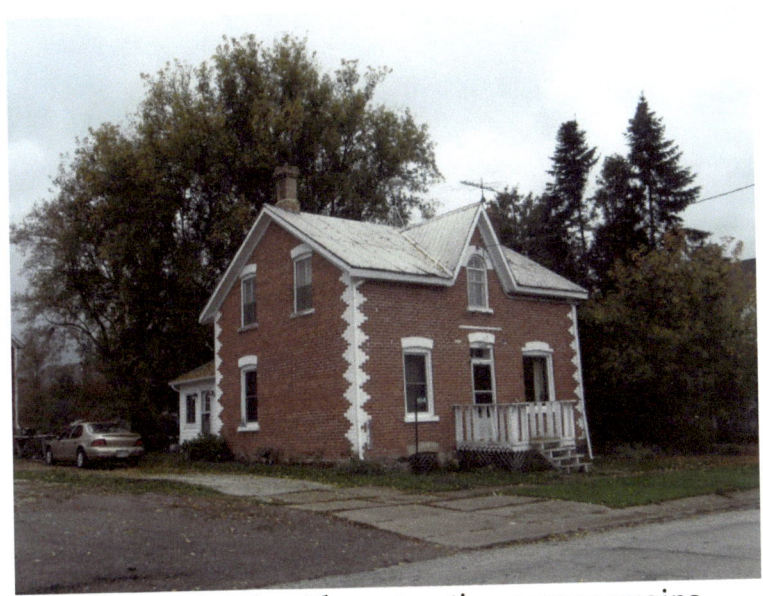

Gothic – brick with contrasting corner quoins

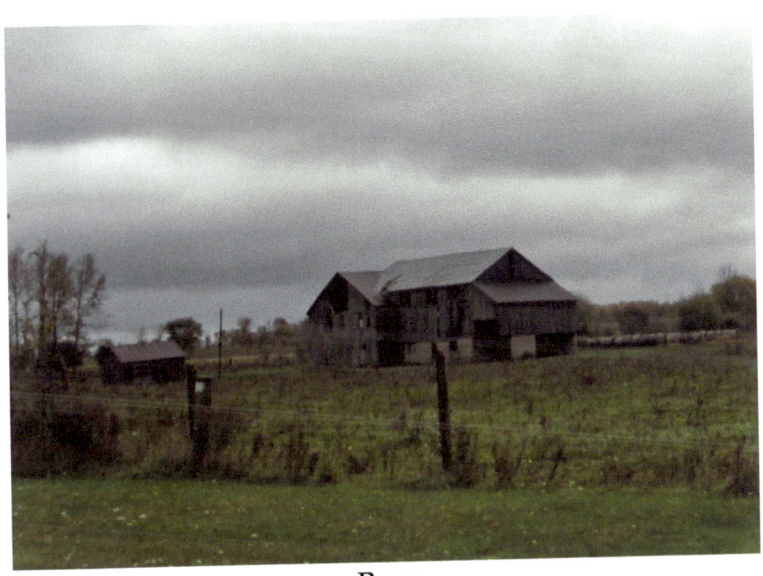

Barn

Meaford

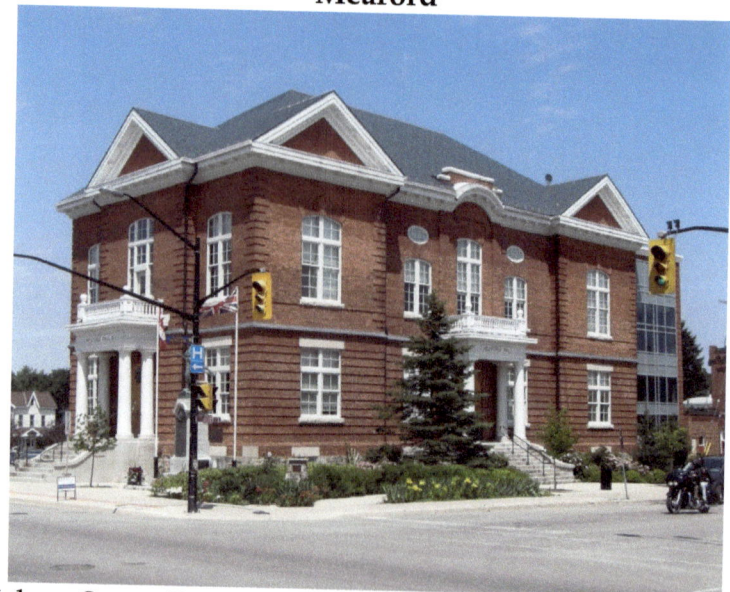

12 Nelson Street East - Meaford Hall – second floor balconies, pediments

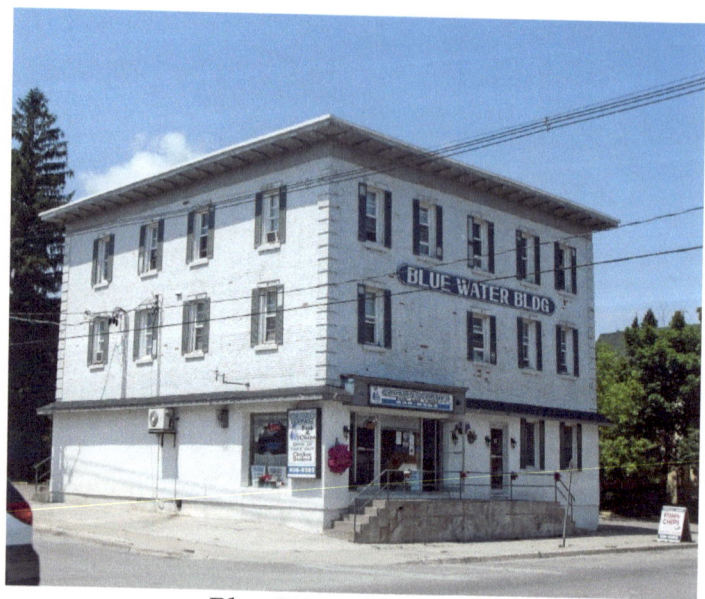

Blue Water Building

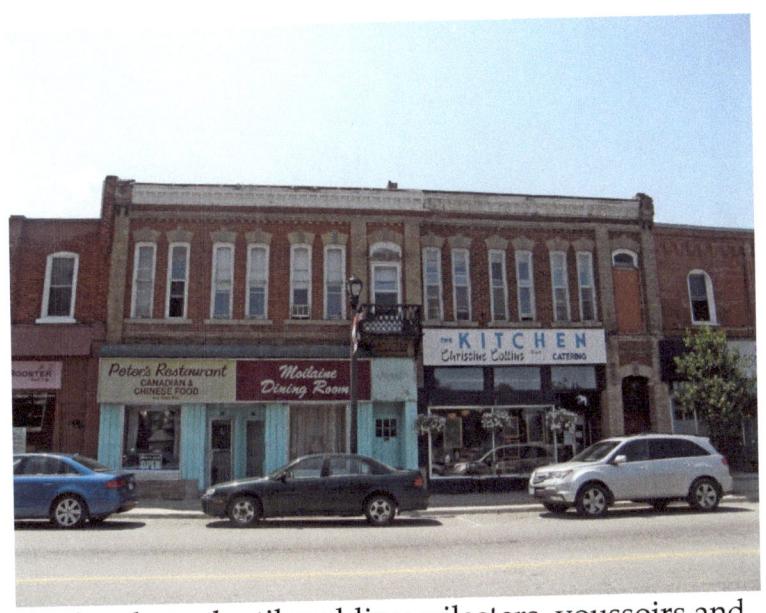

Cornice brackets, dentil molding, pilasters, voussoirs and keystones

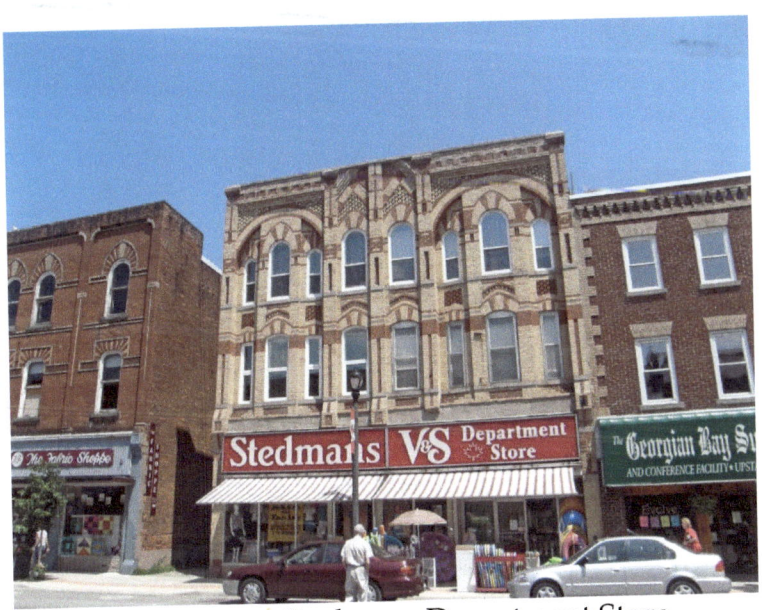

29 North Sykes Street – Stedmans Department Store - pilasters, dichromatic brickwork

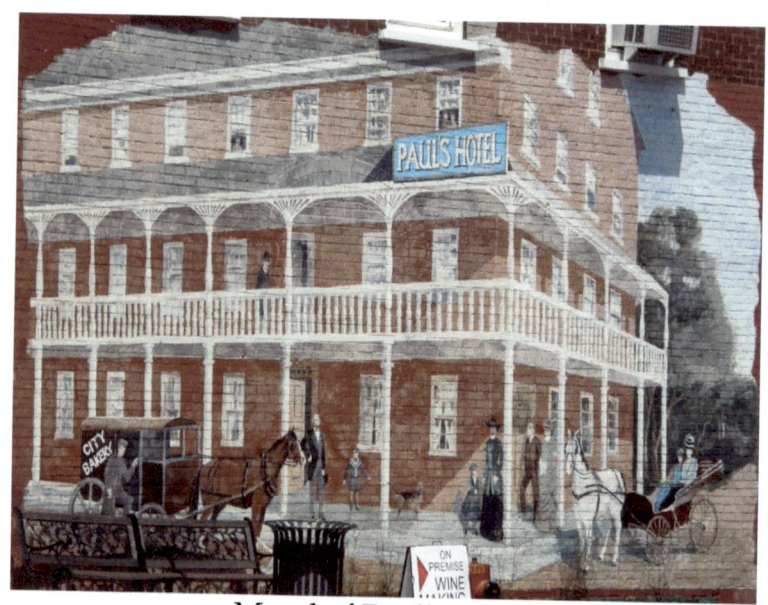
Mural of Paul's Hotel

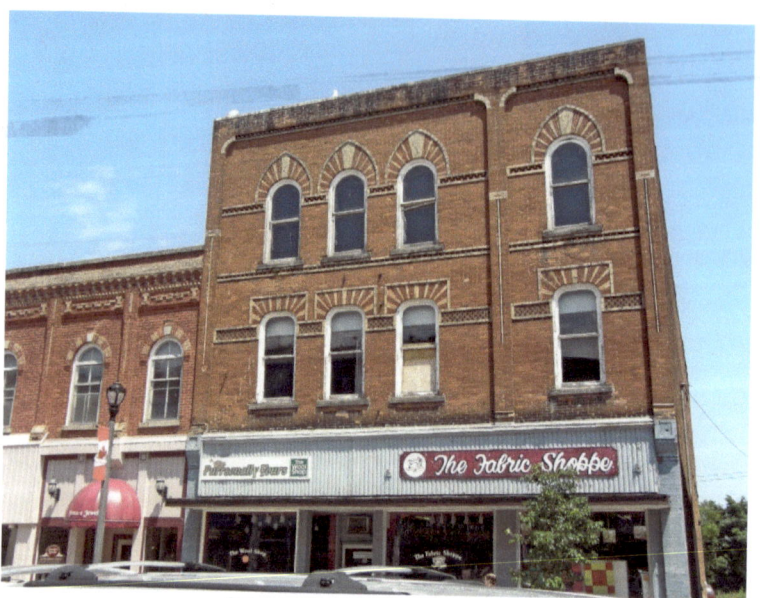
35 North Sykes Street

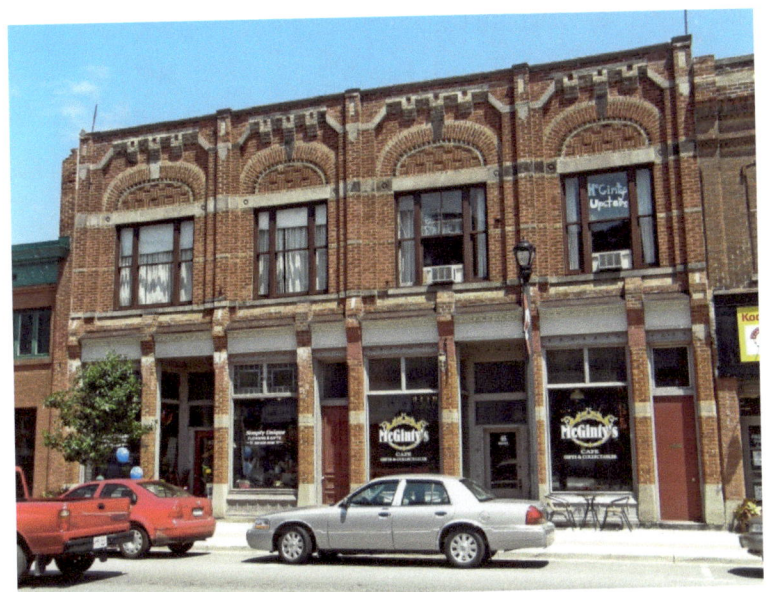

Dichromatic brickwork, pilasters

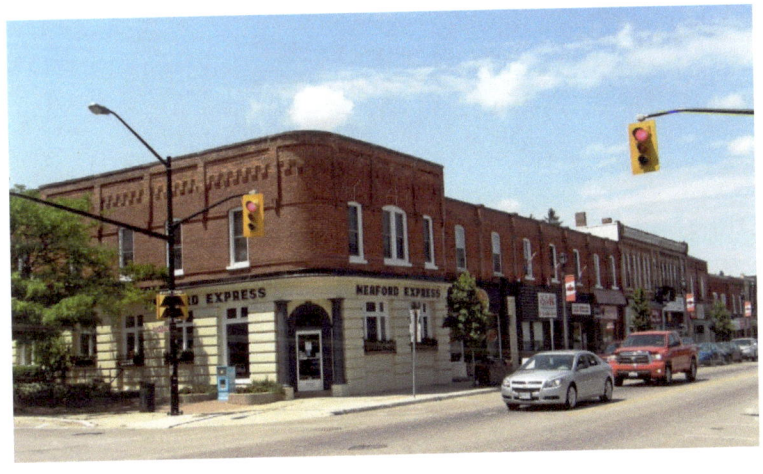

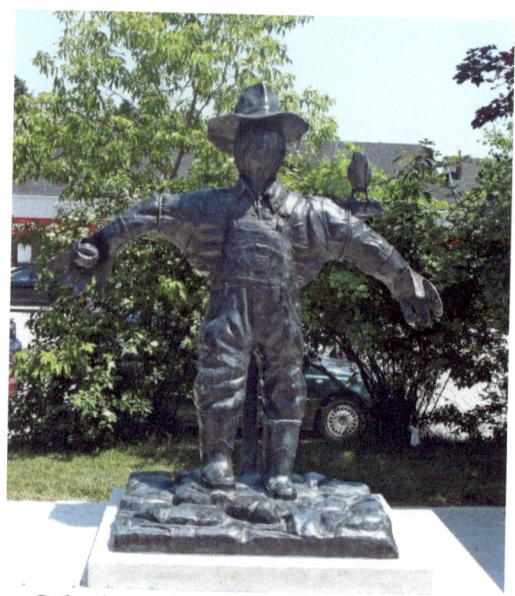

Schubird – Welcome to Meaford

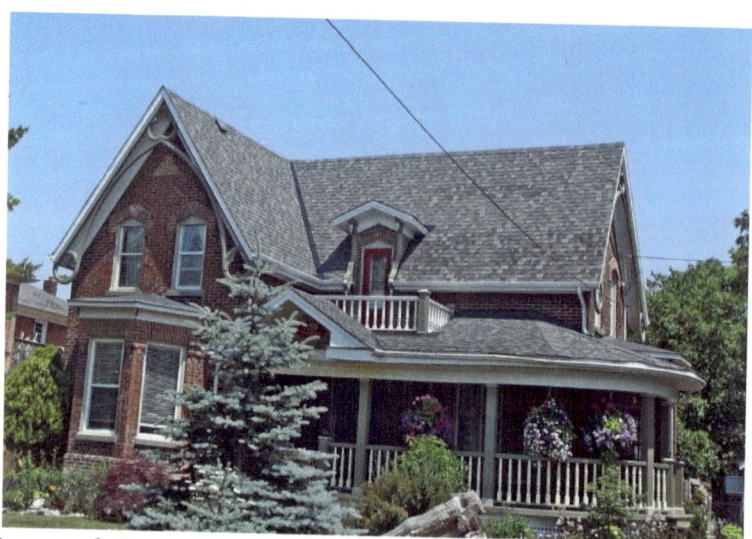

59 Denmark Street - Gothic – dormer leading to second floor balcony, bay window, wraparound veranda

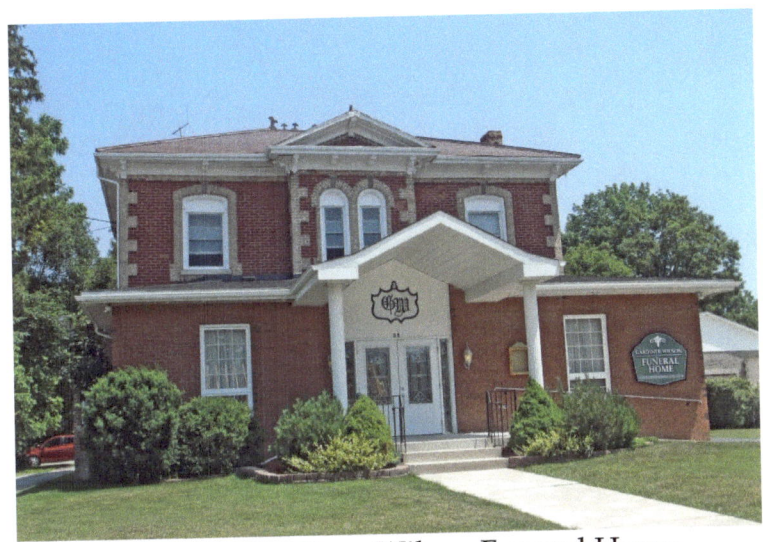

69 Denmark Street - Gardiner-Wilson Funeral Home – frontispiece topped with pediment, corner quoins, hipped roof

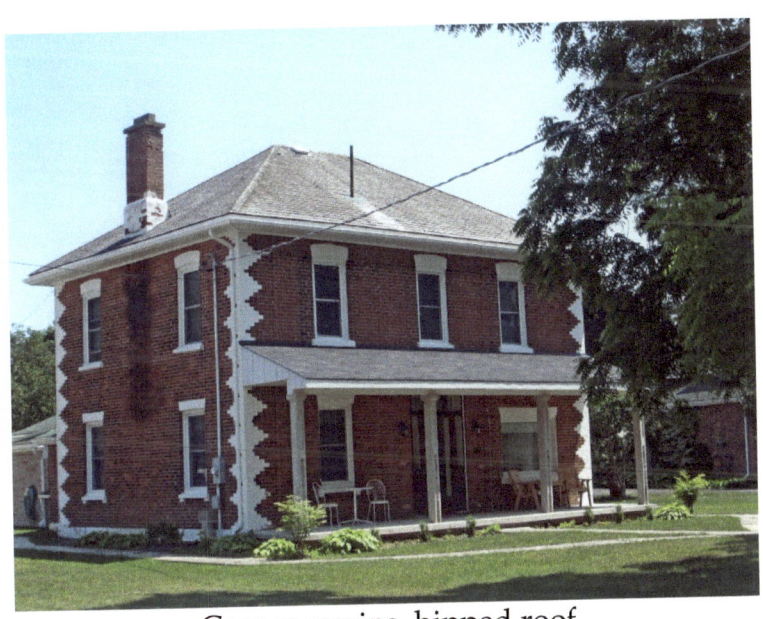

Corner quoins, hipped roof

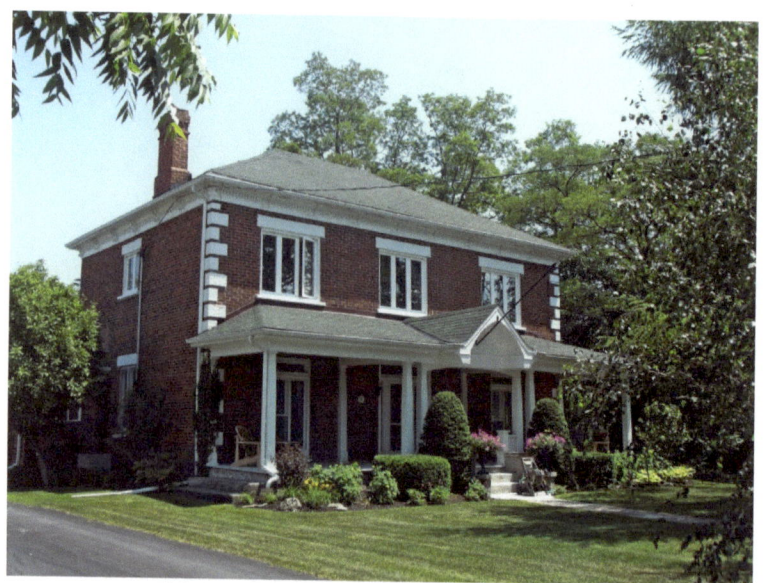
#91 - corner quoins, hipped roof

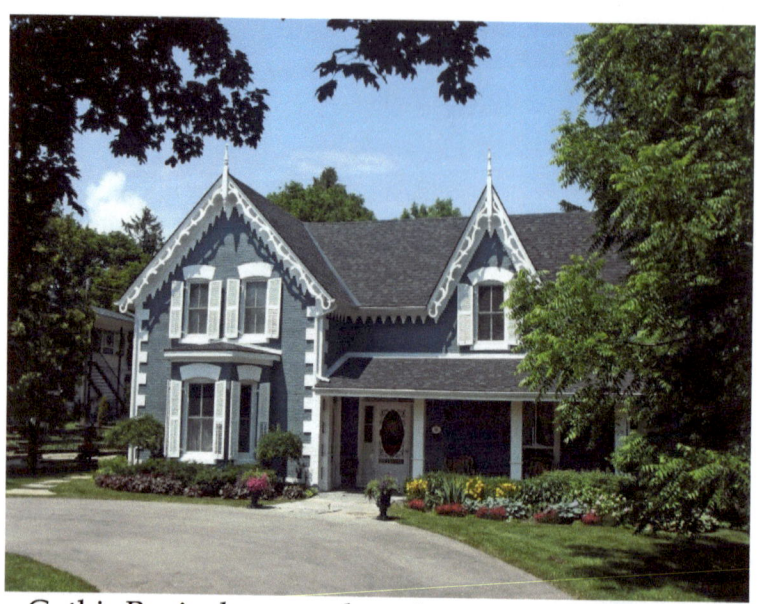
#60 – Gothic Revival – verge board trim and finials on gables, corner quoins

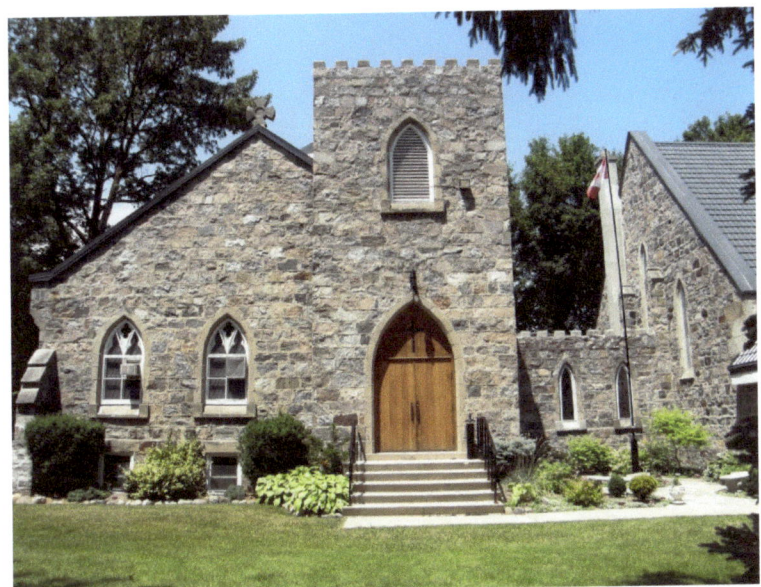

34 Boucher Street East - Christ Church Anglican – stone, tower with battlement

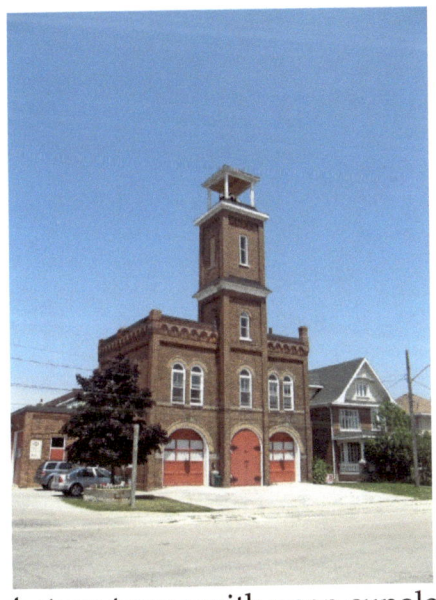

4-story tower with open cupola

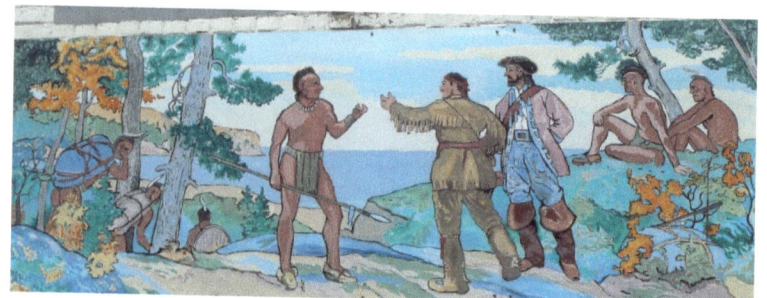
Mural of native Indians meeting explorers

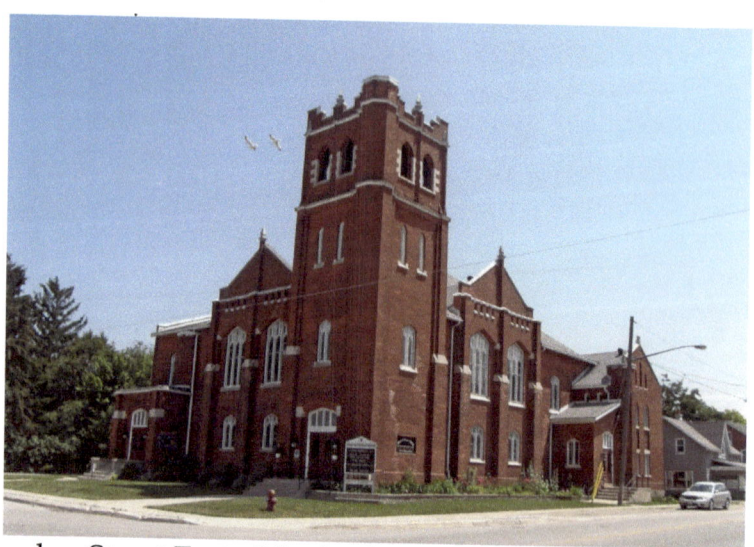
7 Boucher Street East - Meaford United Church – 4-story tower with battlement, windows with muntins

Thornbury

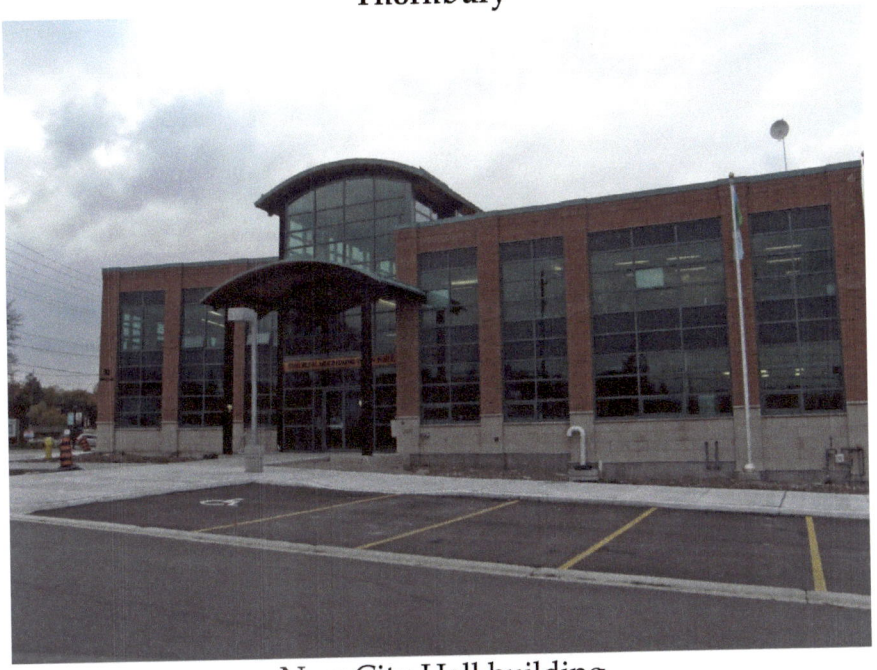

New City Hall building

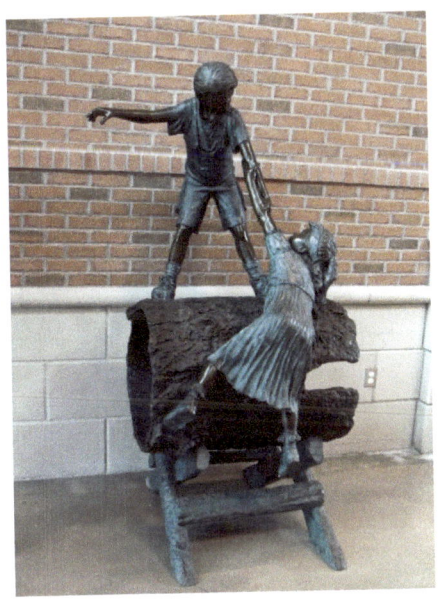

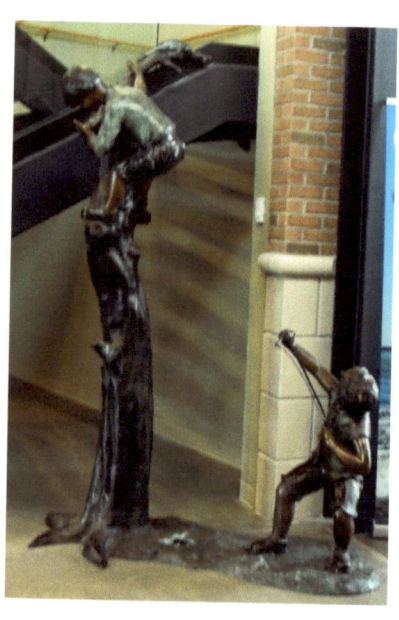

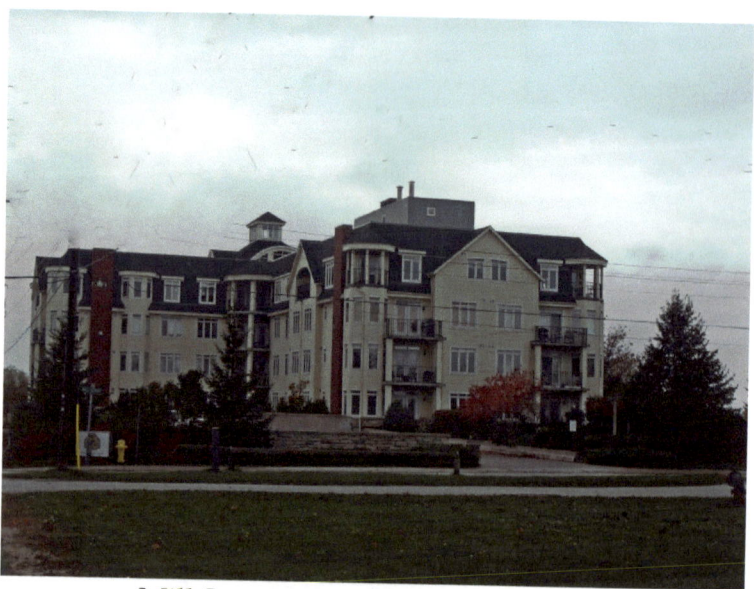
Mill Street apartment with cupola

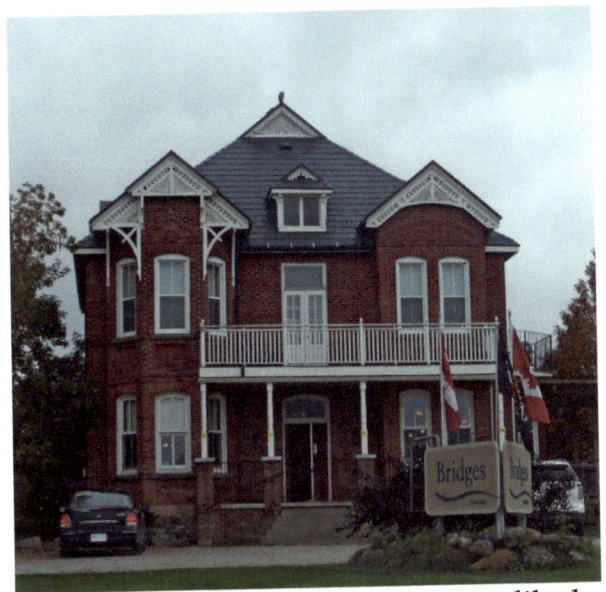

27 Bridge Street - Bridges Tavern – two tower-like bays with verge board trim on gables and fretwork, second floor balcony, dormer in roof

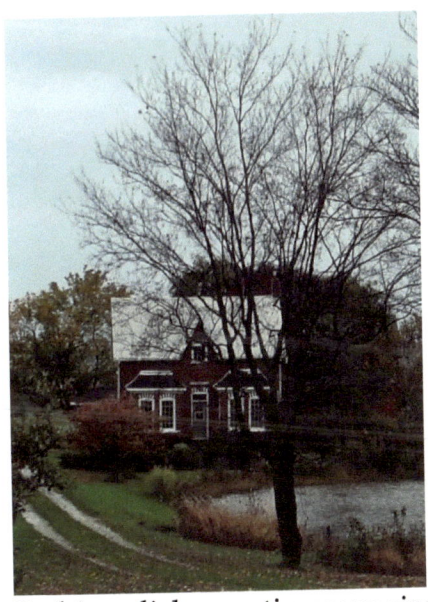

Gothic – dichromatic voussoirs

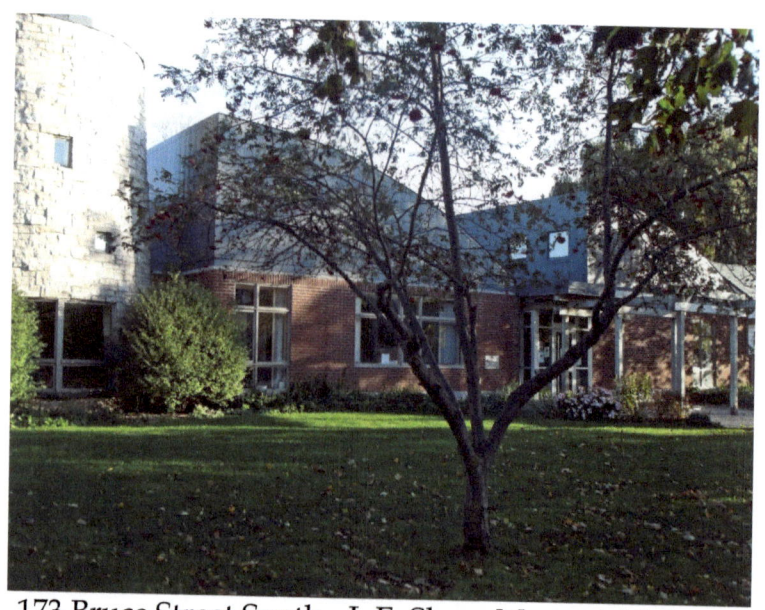
173 Bruce Street South - L.E. Shore Memorial Library

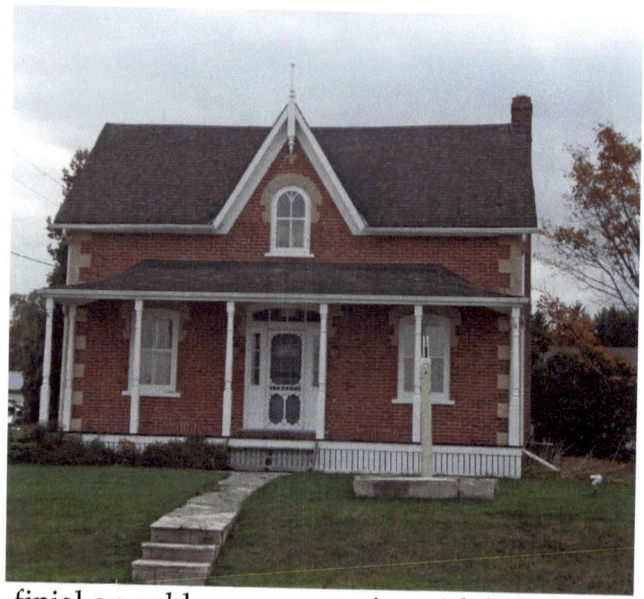
Gothic – finial on gable, corner quoins, sidelights and transom windows around door

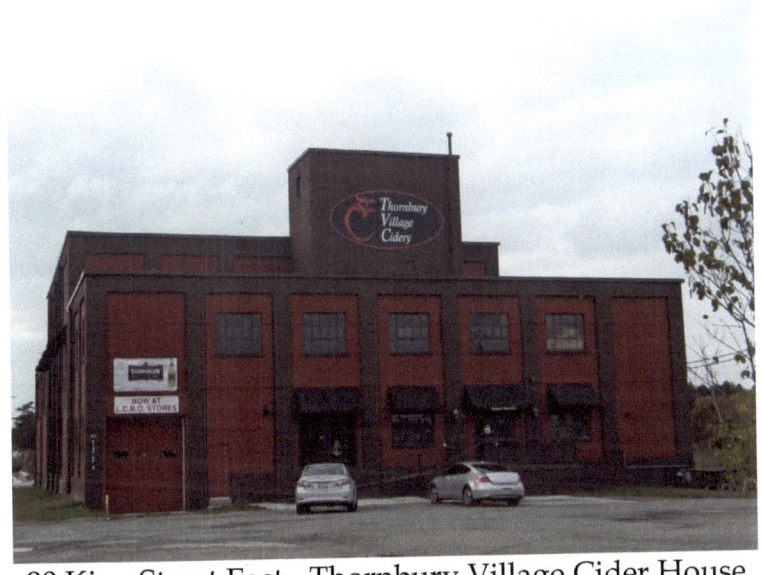

90 King Street East - Thornbury Village Cider House

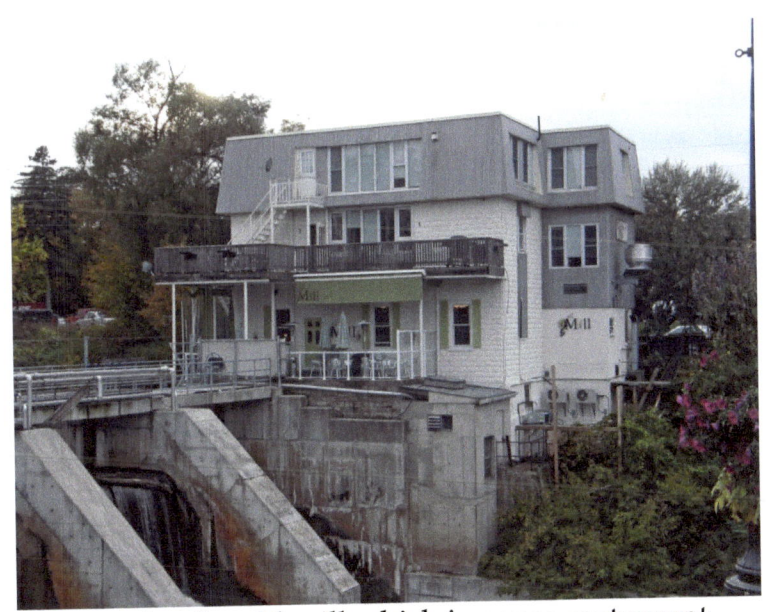

Dam by the old mill which is now a restaurant

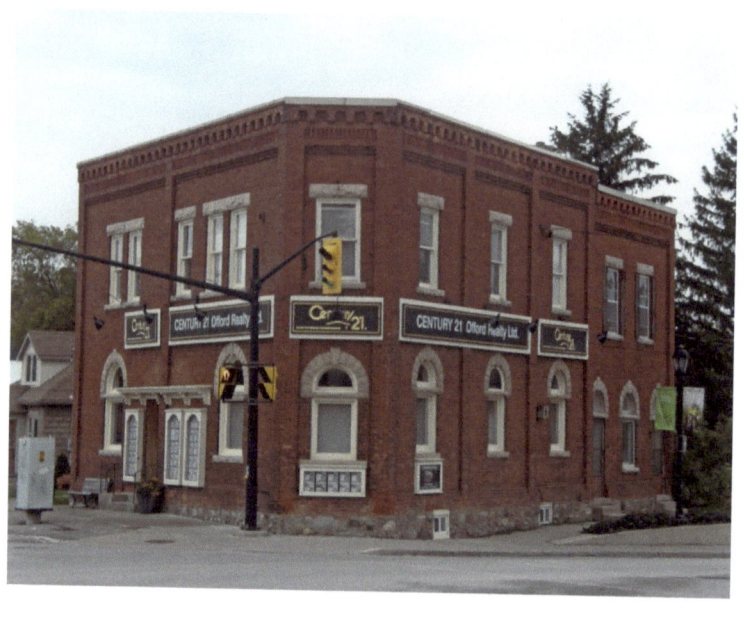

1 Bruce Street North - Dentil molding, voussoirs and keystones

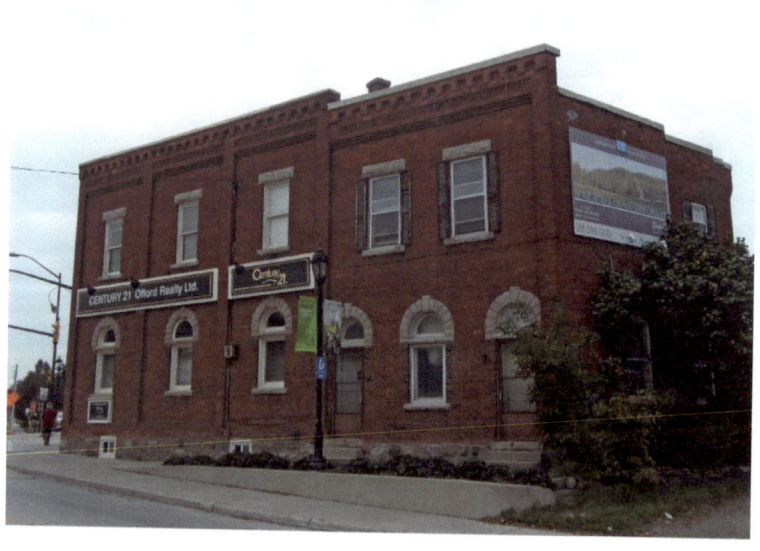

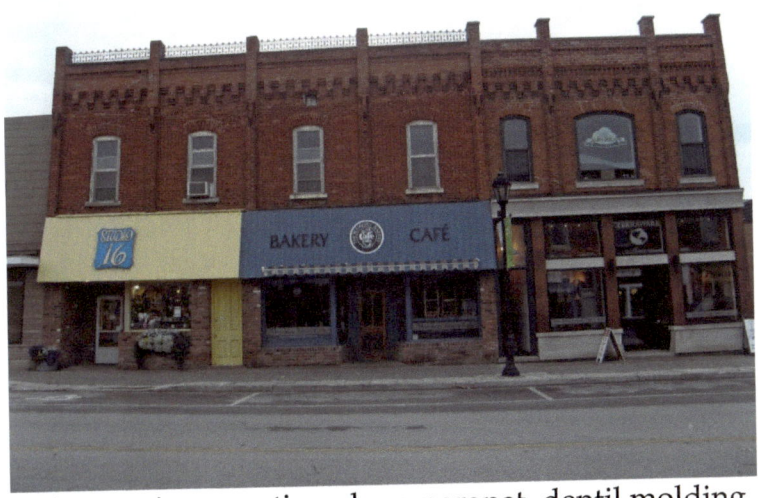

Pilasters, iron cresting along parapet, dentil molding

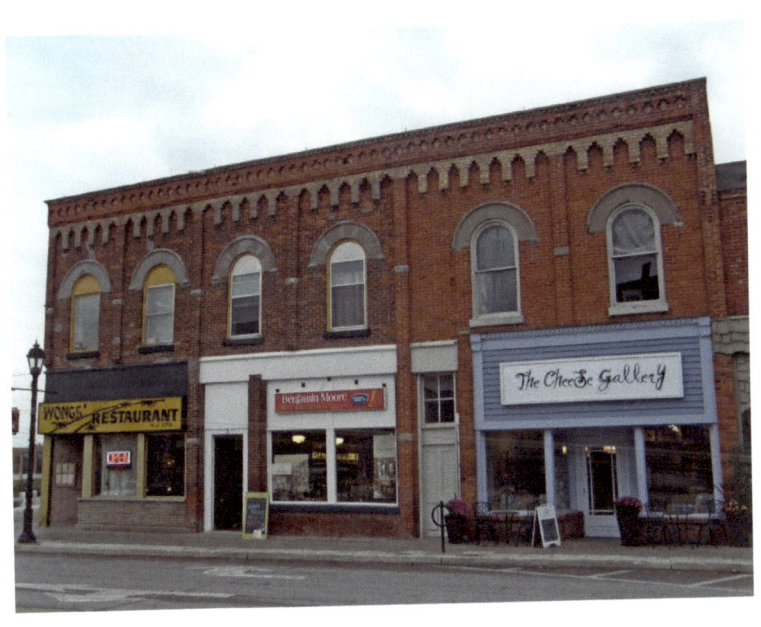

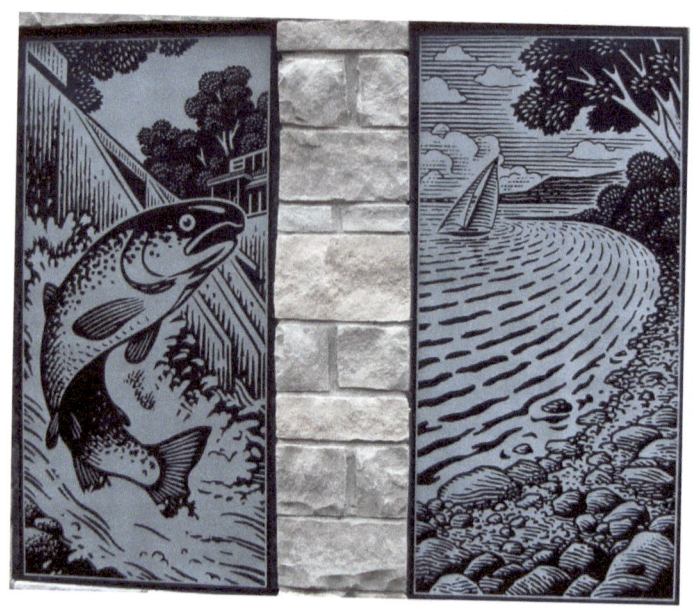

Pictures on the wall

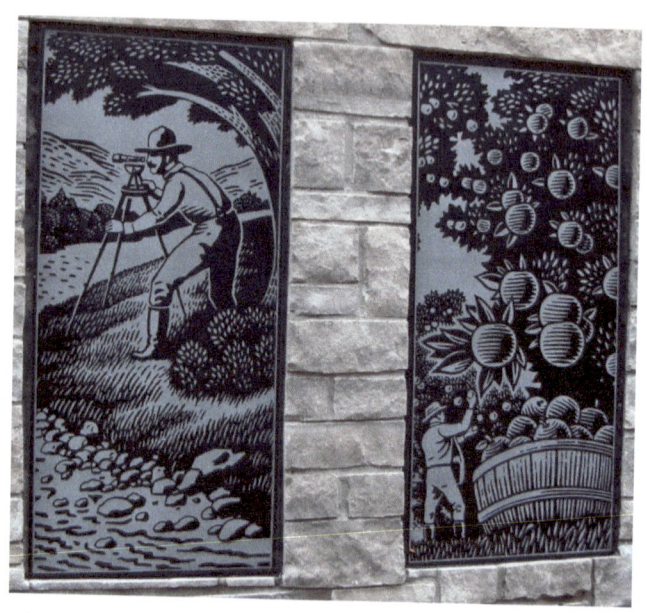

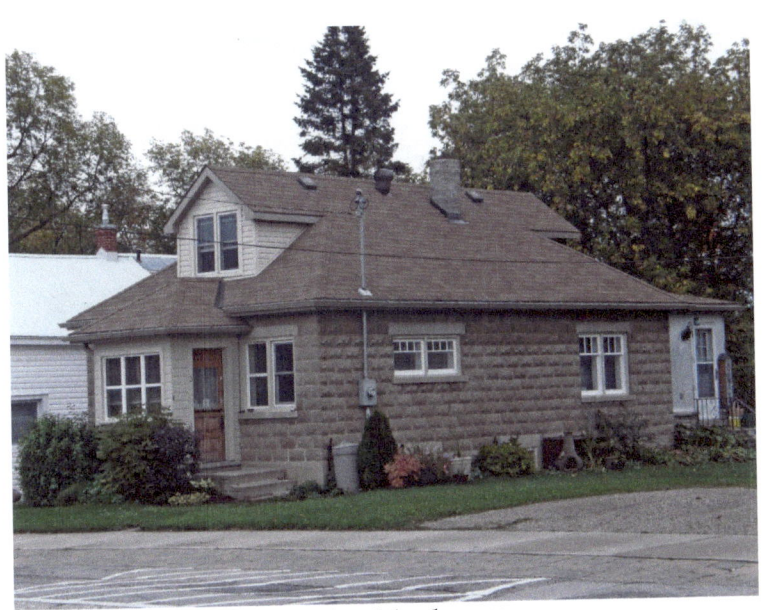

#3 - cinder block cottage

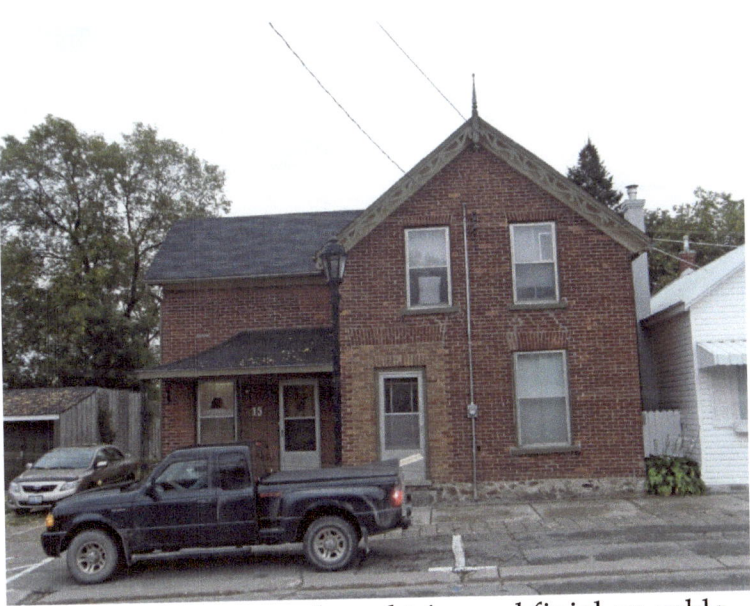

#15 - Gothic – verge board trim and finial on gable

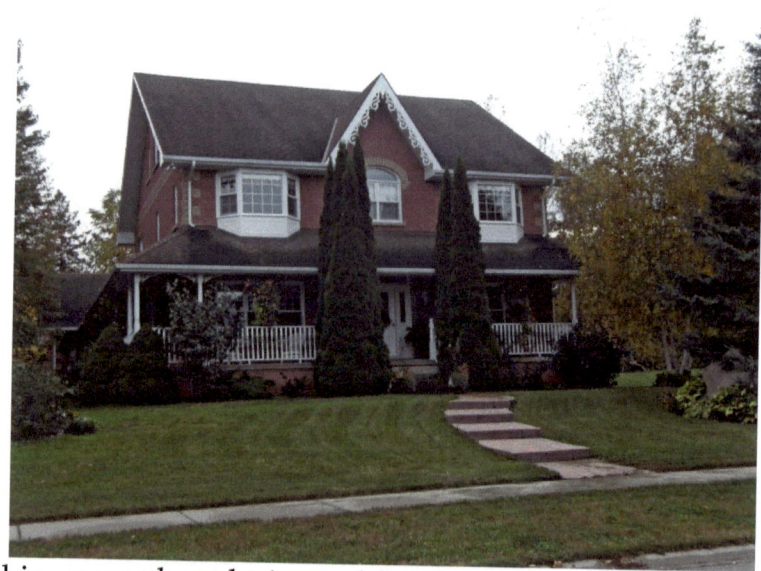

Gothic – verge board trim and finial on gable, wraparound veranda, sidelights, fanlight

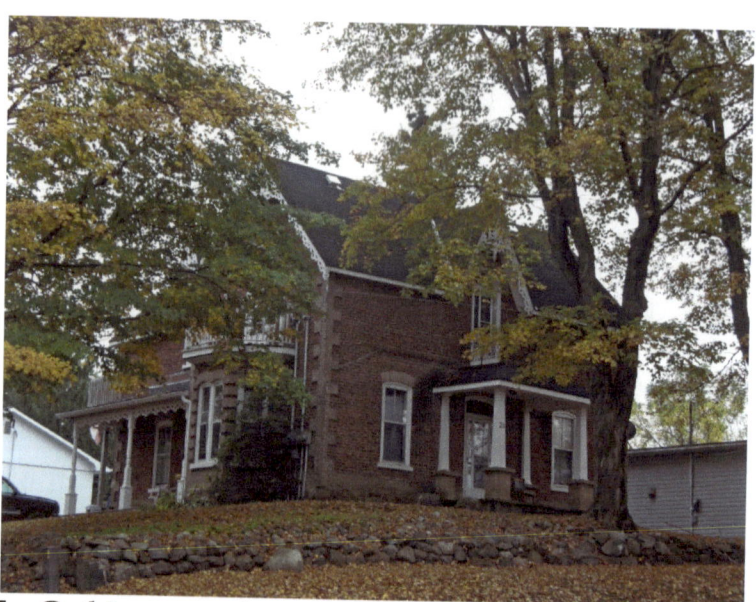

#25 – Gothic – verge board trim and finials on gables, corner quoins

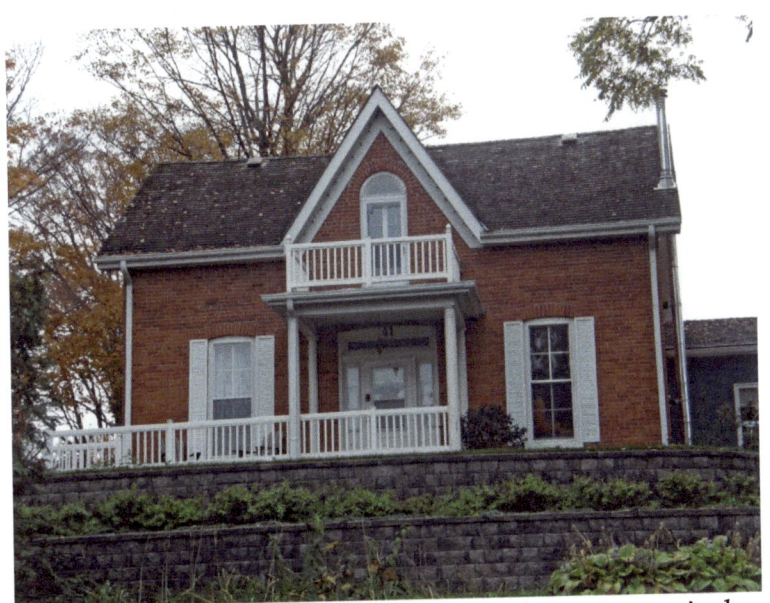

#41 - Second floor balcony, sidelights and transom windows around door with balcony above

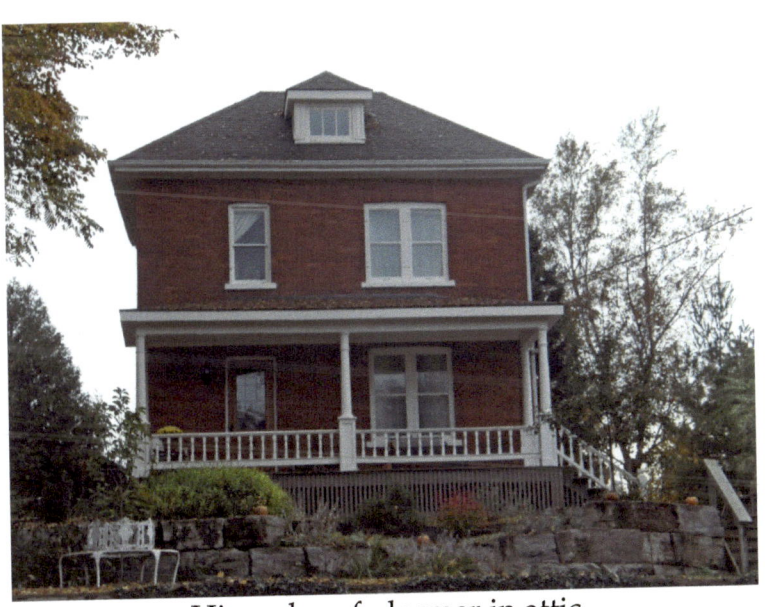

Hipped roof, dormer in attic

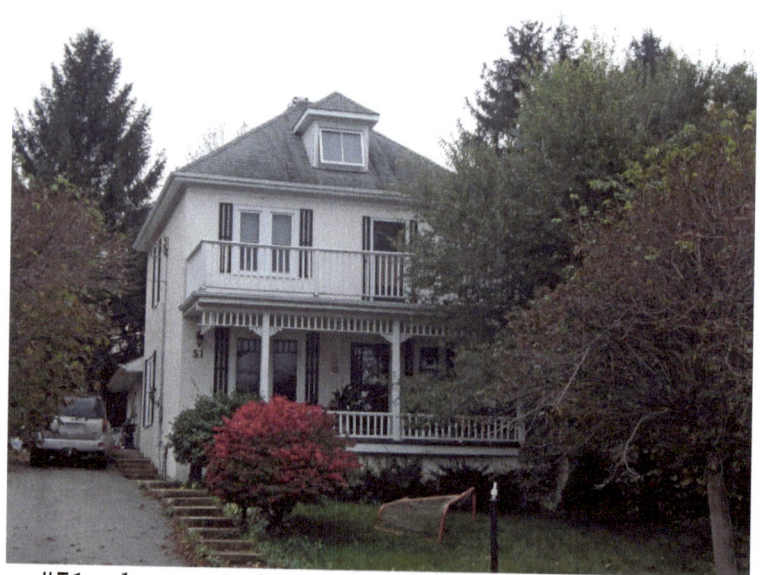
#51 - dormer in hipped roof, second floor balcony

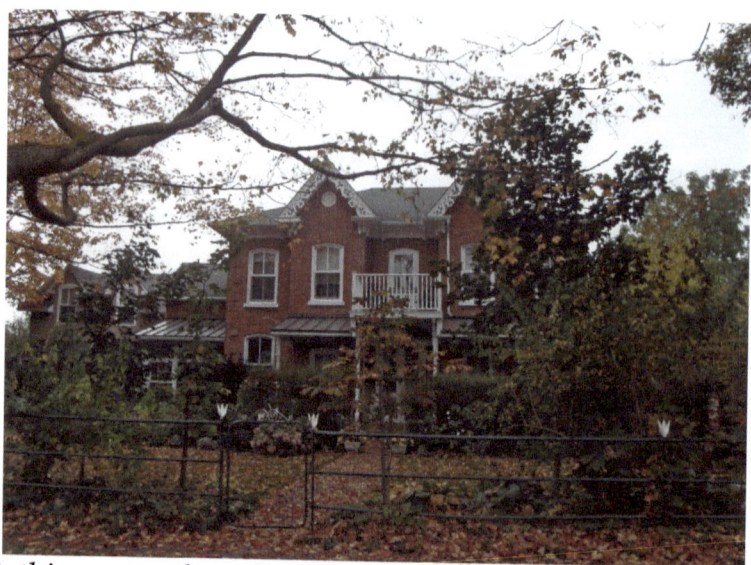
Gothic – verge board trim on gables, second floor balcony

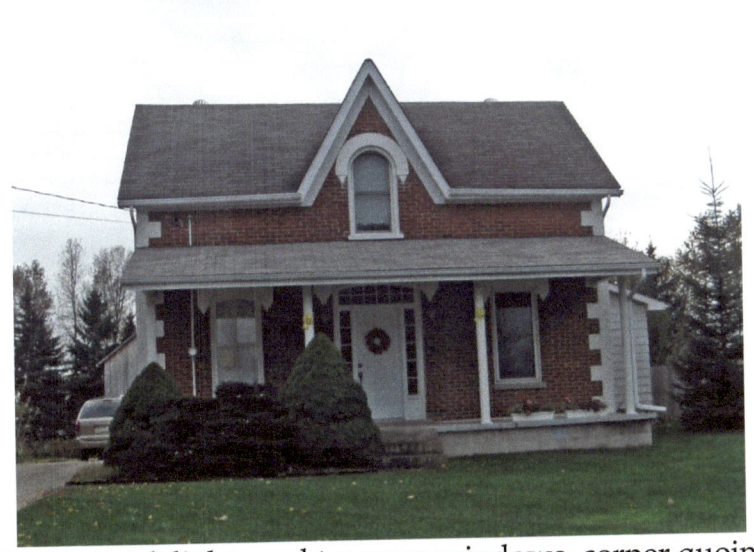

Gothic – sidelights and transom windows, corner quoins

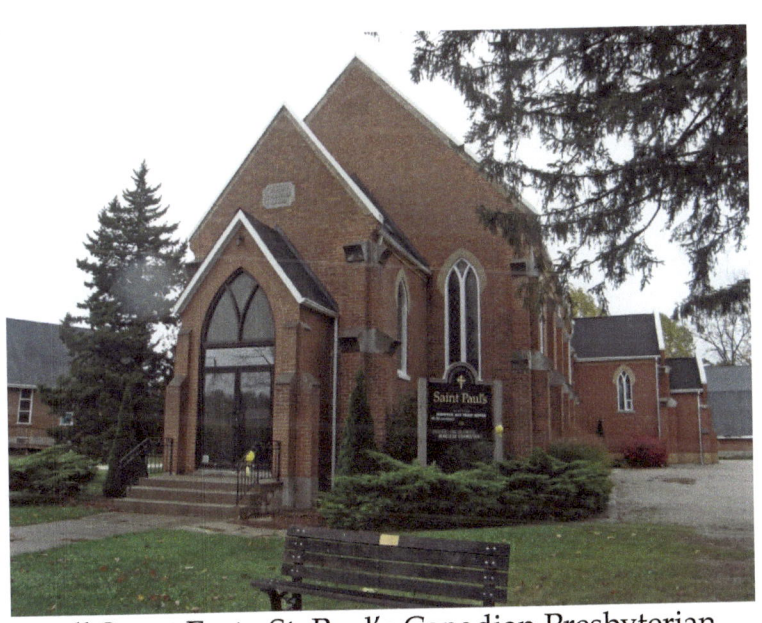

20 Russell Street East - St. Paul's Canadian Presbyterian Church - A.D. 1880

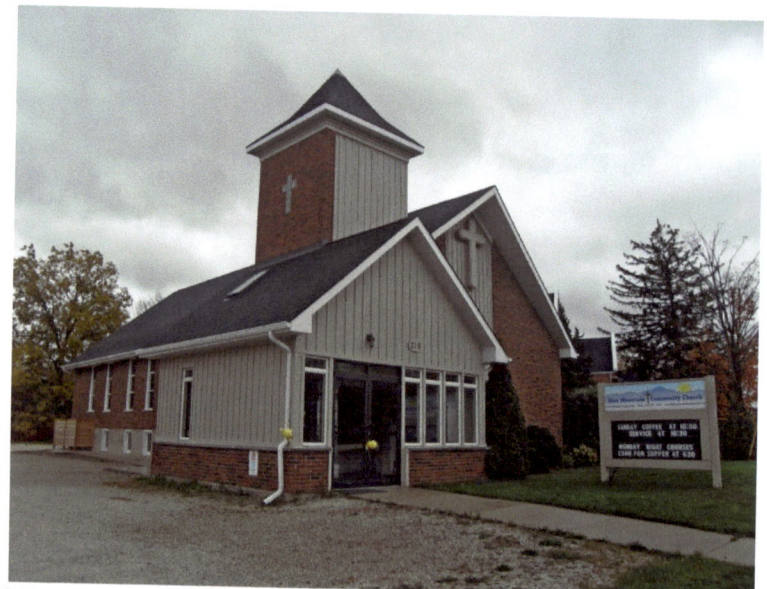

219 Bruce Street South - Blue Mountain Community Church

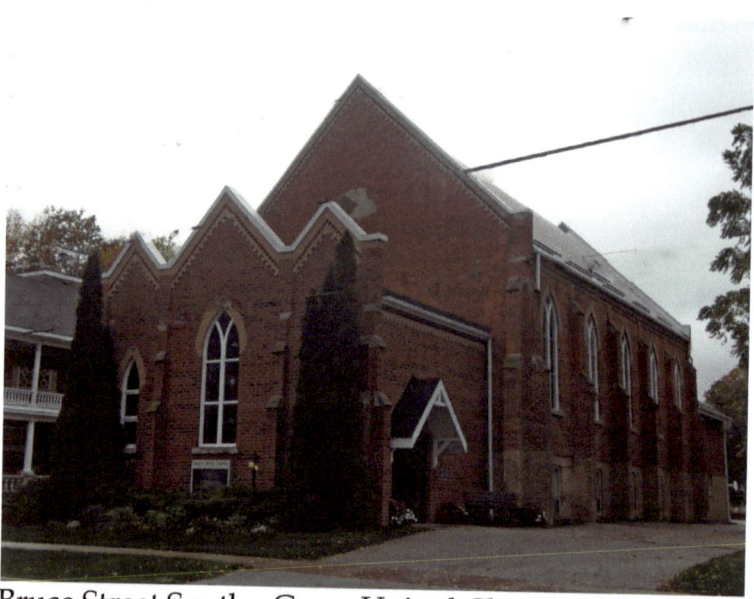

140 Bruce Street South - Grace United Church - former Methodist Church of Canada 1880

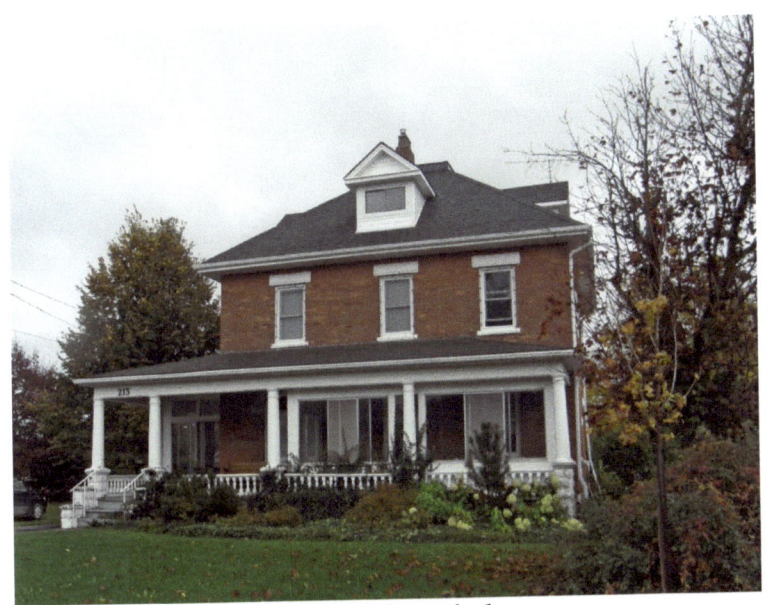

#213 – hipped roof, dormer

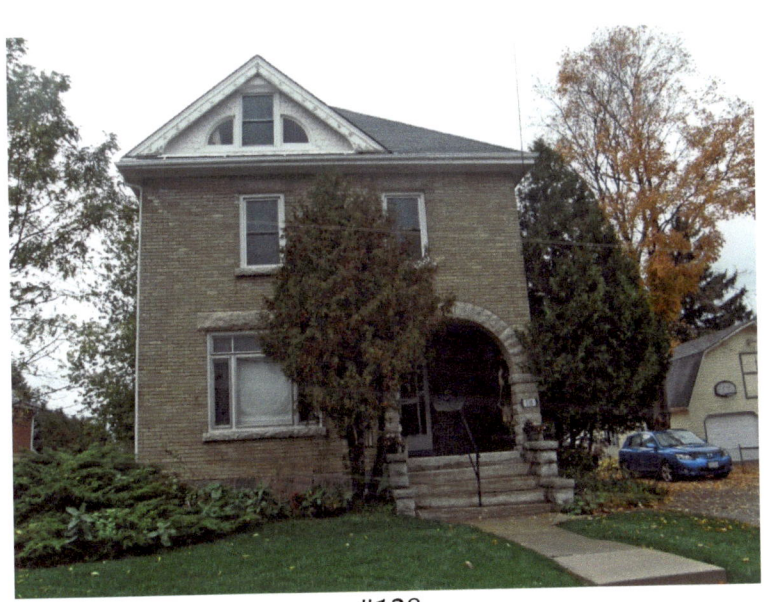

#138

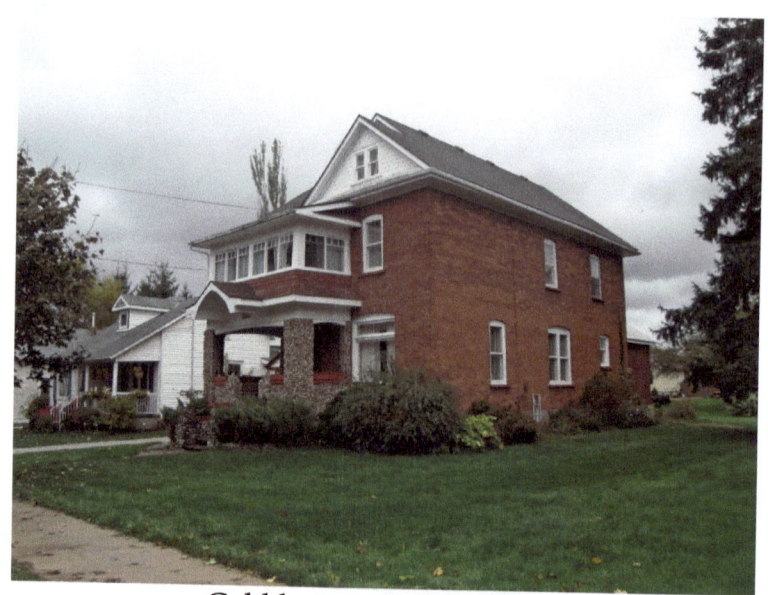

Cobblestone porch pillars

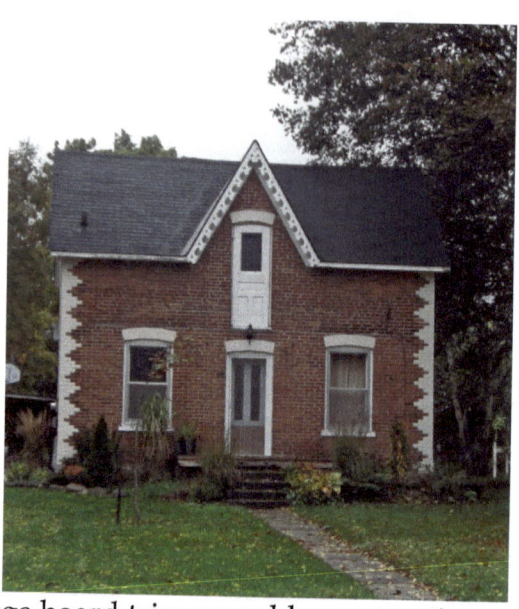

Gothic – verge board trim on gable, contrasting corner quoins

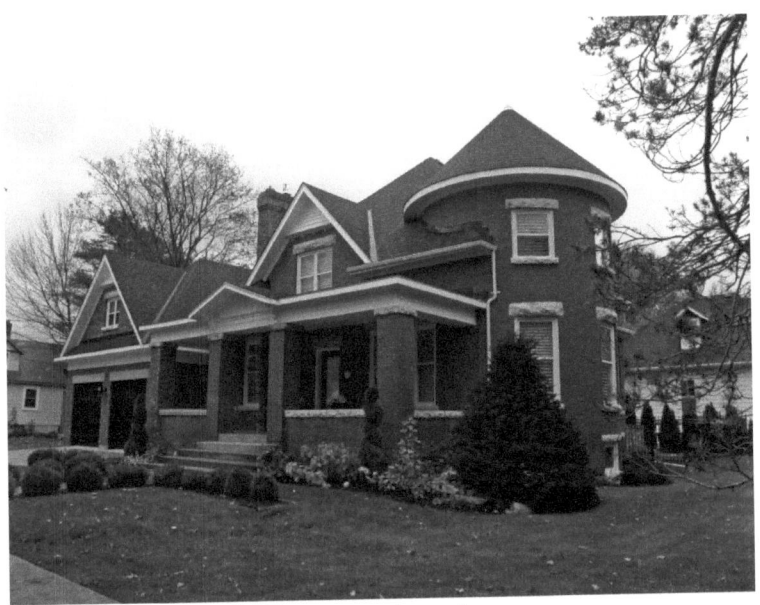

73 – two-story tower

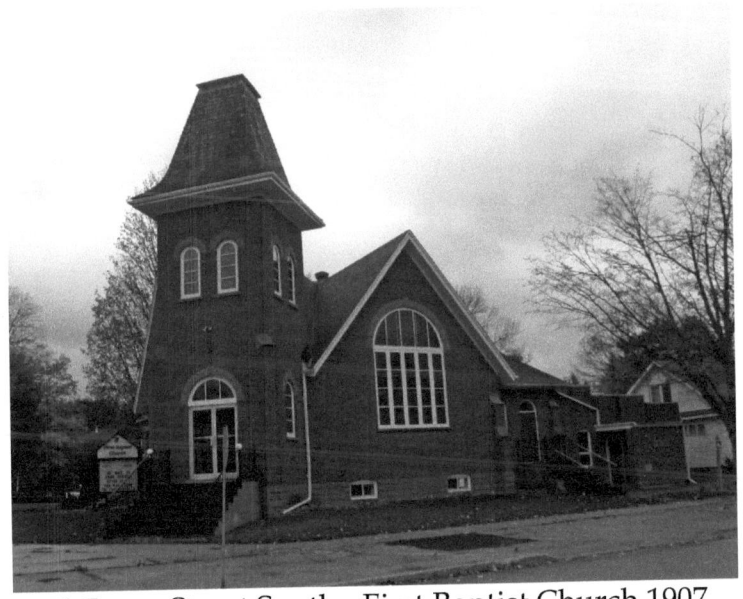

72 Bruce Street South - First Baptist Church 1907

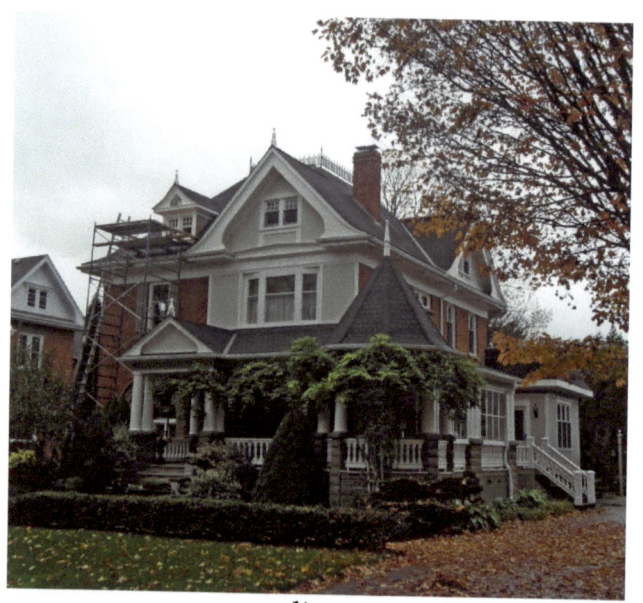
pediment

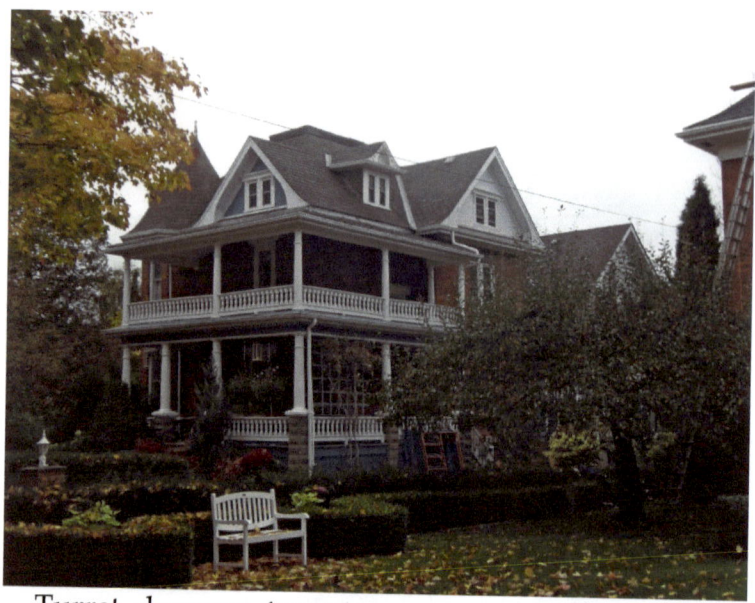
Turret, dormers, two-story wraparound verandas

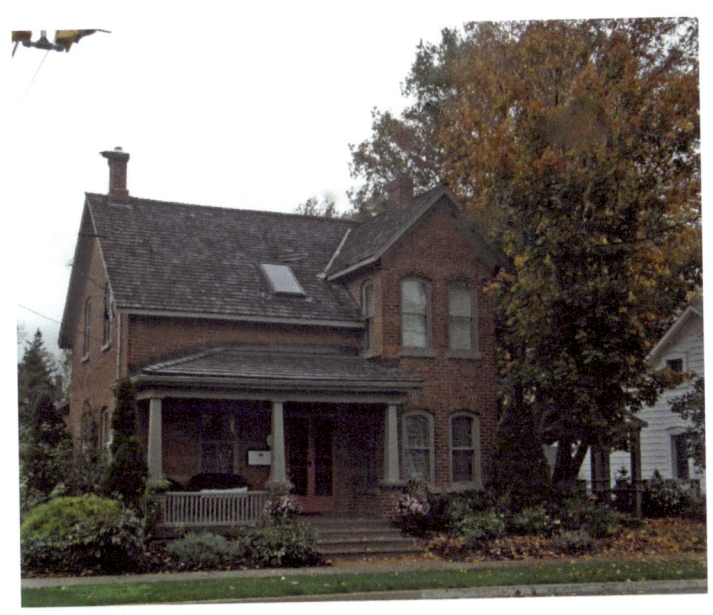

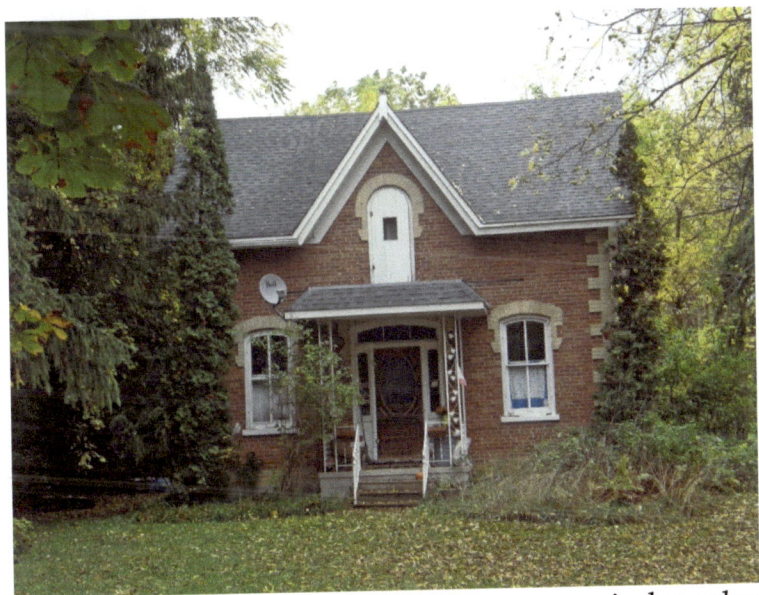

Gothic – corner quoins, sidelights, transom window above door

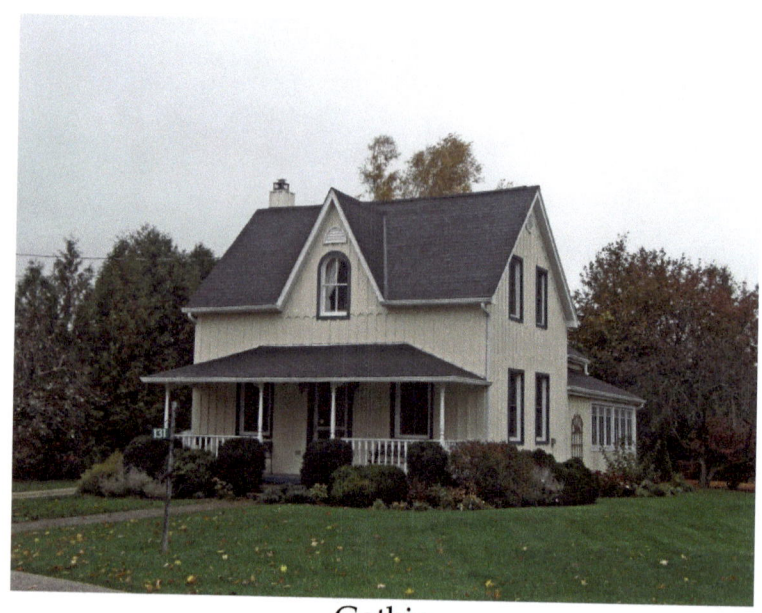

Gothic

Victoria Corners

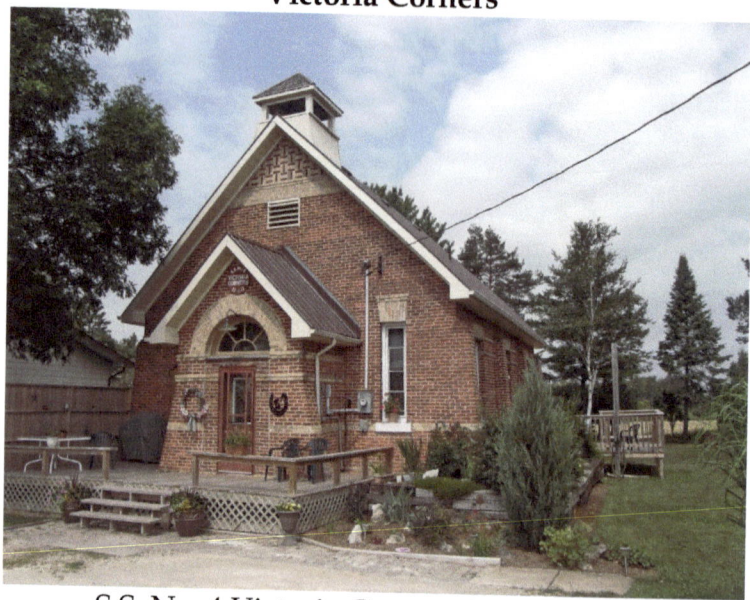

S.S. No. 4 Victoria Corners School – 1880

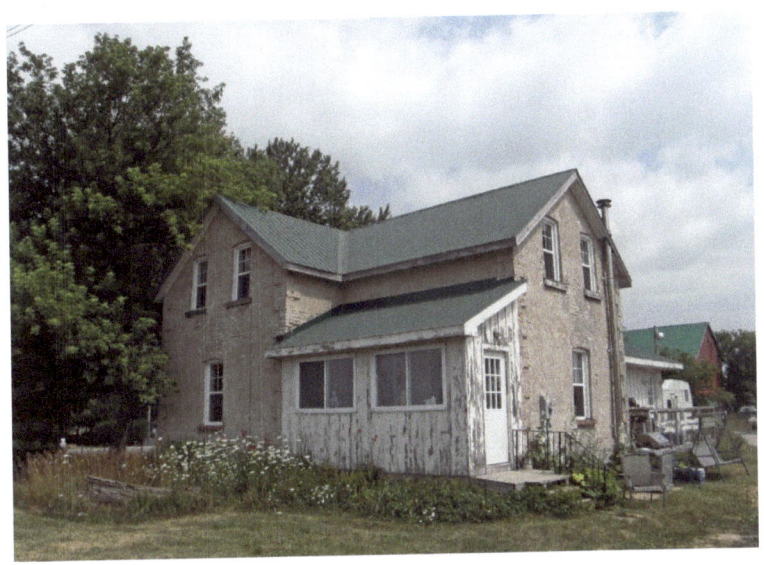

Walter's Falls

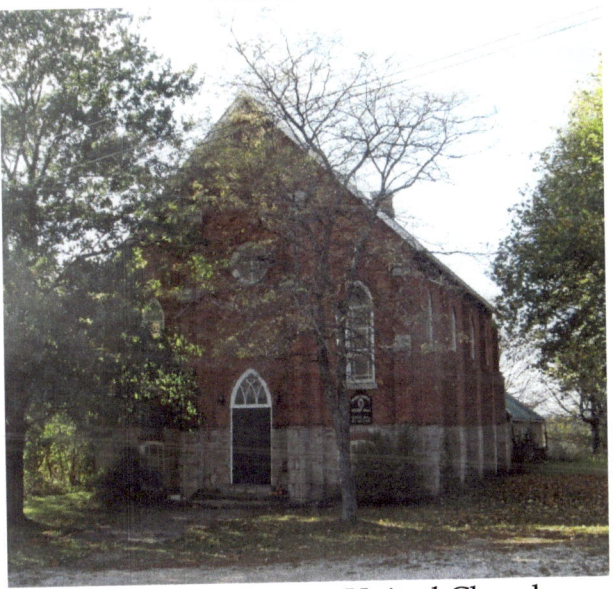

167 Victoria Street - United Church

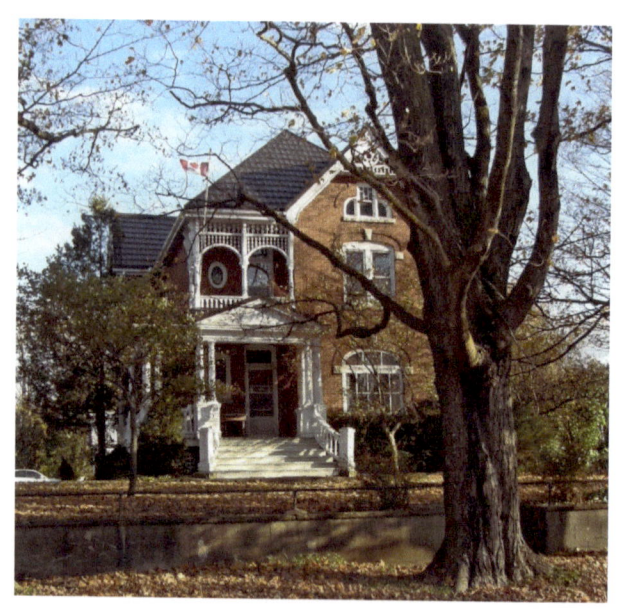

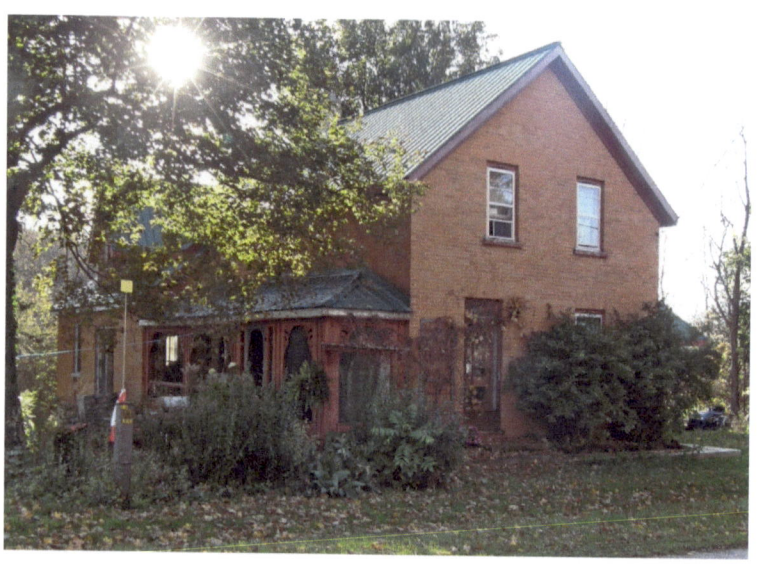

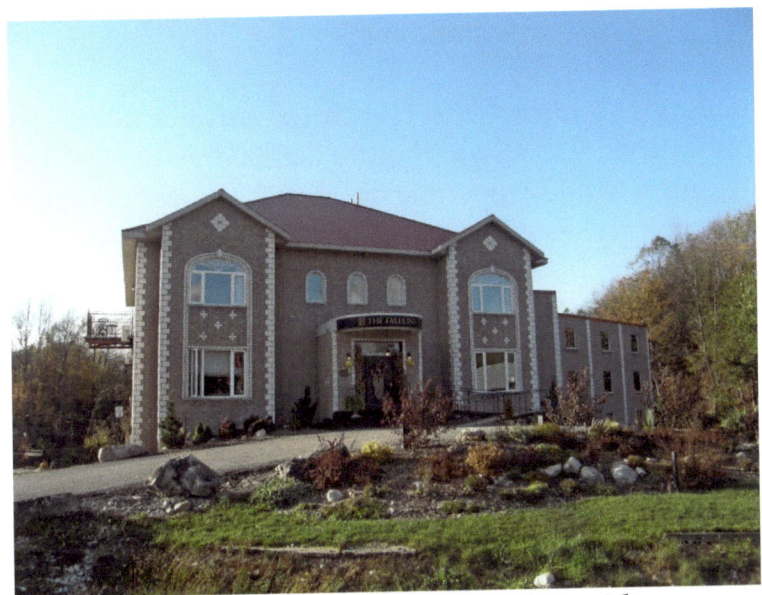

The Falls Inn and Spa – 14-room country inn with spa treatment rooms perched on top of Walter's Falls on the Bruce Trail

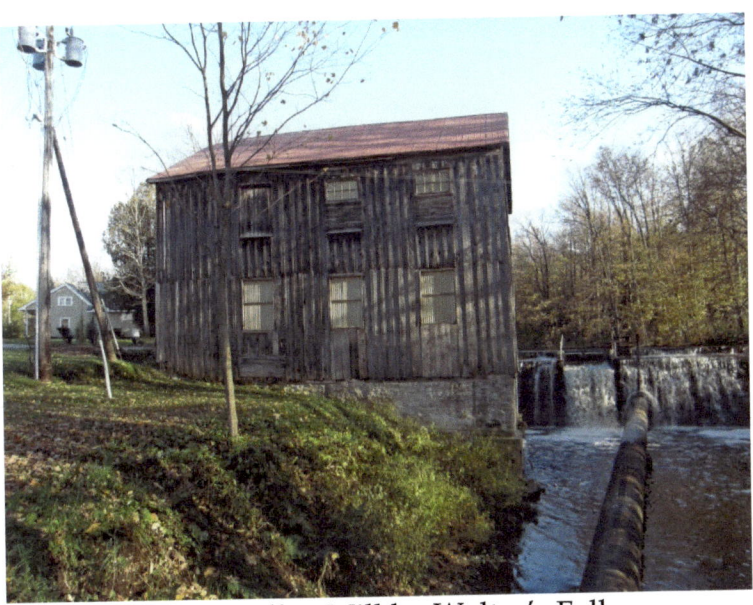

Old Woollen Mill by Walter's Falls

Building Styles

Gothic Revival, 1830-1890 – These decorative buildings have sharply-pitched gables with highly detailed verge boards, pointed-arch window openings, and dichromatic brickwork. It is a common style in Ontario.

Italianate, 1850-1900 – A two story rectangular building with a mild hip roof, a projecting frontispiece, and generous eaves with ornate cornice brackets was the basis of the style; often there are large sash windows, quoins, ornate detailing on the windows, belvederes and wraparound verandahs. Italianate commercial buildings often have cast iron cresting and elegant window surrounds.

Second Empire, 1860-1880 – The mansard roof is the most noteworthy feature of this style and is evidence of the French origins. Projecting central towers and one or two-story bays can also be present.

Other Books by Barbara Raue

Coins of Gold
Arrows, Indians and Love
The Life and Times of Barbara
The Cromwell Family Book
Laura Secord Discovered
Daddy Where Are You?

Montana Series
Book 1: Montana Dream
Book 2: Life on the Montana Frontier
Book 3: Montana to Boston and Back
Book 4: Montana Sons Go to War
Book 5: Montana Sons Return from War

Donaldson Series
Book 1: Rite of Passage
Book 2: Rite of Marriage

© 2021 by Barbara Raue - All the photos in this book have been taken with my cameras. I own the rights to them.

Barbara is The Authority on Saving Our History One Photo at a Time. She is pursuing her interest in photography and architecture by preserving a record through photos of old buildings from the 1800s and 1900s with their unique architecture. Enjoy the beautiful architecture in the comfort of your living room. Dream about what it was like in those bygone days. Dream about what it was like to live in a mansion like one of those in this book.

Barbara Raue, a wife, mother and grandmother, is an avid reader and writer. She has researched and compiled several family histories. In 2010, Barbara published her book "Coins of Gold," which celebrates the courageous life of her mother, May Todd. Barbara's second book is a historical fiction "Arrows, Indians and Love" which takes place in Boonesborough, Kentucky during the time of Daniel Boone. In 2013, Barbara published *The Cromwell Family Book* in which she traces her ancestry generations back into Great Britain. Her second novel is called *Laura Secord Discovered,* in which the story of Laura's service during the War of 1812 is shared. Barbara's memoir is titled *Daddy Where Are You?* It tells of her life growing up without a father. Five novels in the Montana Series have been published, *Montana Dream, Life on the Montana Frontier, Montana to Boston and Back, Montana Sons Go to War,* and *Montana Sons Return from War.* The Donaldson series of two novels is available: *Rite of Passage* and *Rite of Marriage.*

This is a link to Barbara's website to view all of her books
http://barbararaue.ca